Maths — No Problem!

Singapore Maths
English National Curriculum 2014

Consultant and Author
Dr. Yeap Ban Har

UK Consultant
Dr. Anne Hermanson

shinglee

Published by Maths — No Problem!
Copyright © 2018 by Maths — No Problem!

Printed in the United Kingdom
First Printing, 2016
Reprinted once in 2016, once in 2017 and in 2018

ISBN 978-1-910504-22-2

Maths — No Problem!
Dowding House, Coach & Horses Passage
Tunbridge Wells, UK TN2 5NP

www.mathsnoproblem.com

Acknowledgements

This Maths — No Problem! series, adapted from the New Syllabus
Primary Mathematics series, is published in collaboration with
Shing Lee Publishers. Pte Ltd. The publisher would like to thank
Dr. Tony Gardiner for his contribution.

Design and Illustration by Kin

Preface

Maths — No Problem! is a comprehensive series that adopts a spiral design with carefully built-up mathematical concepts and processes adapted from the maths mastery approaches used in Singapore. The Concrete-Pictorial-Abstract (C-P-A) approach forms an integral part of the learning process through the materials developed for this series.

Maths — No Problem! incorporates the use of concrete aids and manipulatives, problem-solving and group work.

In Maths — No Problem! Primary 6, these features are exemplified throughout the chapters:

Chapter Opener

Familiar events or occurrences that serve as an introduction for pupils.

In Focus

Includes questions related to various lesson objectives as an introductory activity for pupils.

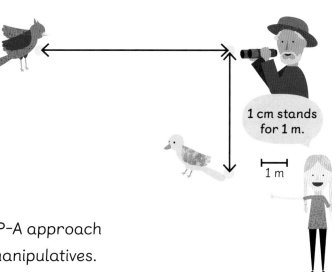

Let's Learn

Introduces new concepts through a C-P-A approach with the use of engaging pictures and manipulatives. Guided examples are provided for reinforcement.

Activity Time

Provides pupils with opportunities to work as individuals or in small groups to explore mathematical concepts or to play games.

Guided Practice

Comprises questions for further consolidation and for the immediate evaluation of pupils' learning.

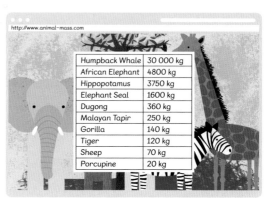

Mind Workout

Challenging non-routine questions for pupils to apply relevant heuristics and to develop higher-order thinking skills.

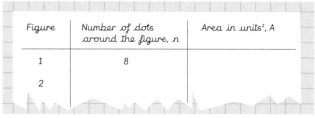

Maths Journal

Provides pupils with opportunities to show their understanding of the mathematical concepts learnt.

Self Check

Allows pupils to assess their own learning after each chapter.

I know how to...

☐ compare quantities and numbers using ratios.

☐ solve problems involving ratios.

Contents

Chapter 10   Area and Perimeter

Chapter 11   Volume

Chapter 14 Graphs and Averages Page

Chapter 15 Negative Numbers

Chapter 7
Percentage

Finding the Percentage of a Number

In Focus

The rules for a sports competition state that no more than 40% of each team can be Year 6 pupils.

Team Alpha	Team Beta	Team Gamma
50 participants	65 participants	42 participants

Find the greatest number of Year 6 pupils allowed in each team.

Let's Learn

1 40% of 50 =

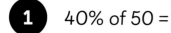

10% ⟶ 50 ÷ 10 = 5

40% ⟶ 4 × 5 = 20

Team Alpha can have up to 20 Year 6 pupils.

2   40% of 65 =

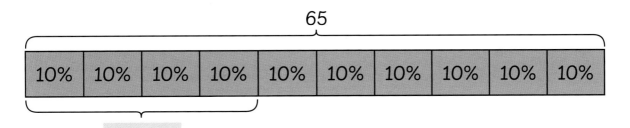

10% ⟶ 65 ÷ 10 = 6.5

40% ⟶ 4 × 6.5 = 26

Team Beta can have up to 26 Year 6 pupils.

3   40% of 42 =

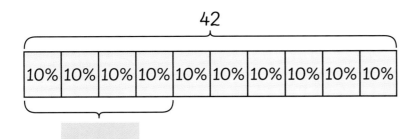

10% ⟶ 42 ÷ 10 = 4.2

40% ⟶ 4 × 4.2 = 16.8

Team Gamma can have up to 16 Year 6 pupils.

This table shows the results of a survey among Year 6 pupils.

Ice cream flavours	Per cent choosing as favourite
chocolate	40%
vanilla	35%
strawberry	10%
others	15%

80 pupils were surveyed.

(a)   10% of 80 = ⬜

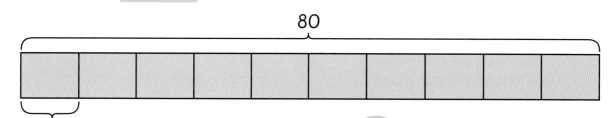

(b)   40% of 80 = ⬜

10% ⟶ ⬜
40% ⟶ ⬜

(c)   15% of 80 = ⬜

10% ⟶ ⬜
5% ⟶ ⬜
15% ⟶ ⬜

(d)   35% of 80 = ⬜

Complete Worksheet **1** – Page **1 - 2**

Finding the Percentage of a Quantity

In Focus

Ingredients for lemonade

6 cups (1.35 l) cold water
2 cups (450 ml) lemon syrup
a pinch of salt

 mixes the cold water and the lemon syrup. Out of 100, how many parts of the mixture is lemon syrup?

Let's Learn

1

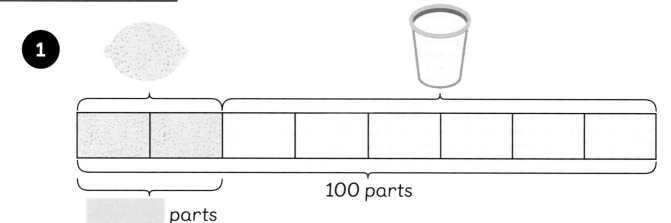

100 parts

parts

$100 \div 4 = 25$

25 out of 100 parts of the mixture is lemon syrup.

25% of the mixture is lemon syrup.

That means for every 100 ml of mixture, 25 ml is lemon syrup.

2 wants to prepare a 2-litre batch of lemonade. How much lemon syrup does he need?

> 2 l = 2000 ml

Method 1

For every 100 ml, needs 25 ml of lemon syrup.

For every 1000 ml, needs 250 ml of lemon syrup.

For every 2000 ml, needs 500 ml of lemon syrup.

Method 2

2 l

| 25% | 25% | 25% | 25% |

$$2\ l \div 4 = 2000\ ml \div 4$$
$$= 500\ ml$$

Method 3

$$25\%\ of\ 2\ l = \frac{25}{100} \times 2000\ ml$$

$$= \frac{1}{4} \times 2000\ ml$$

$$= 500\ ml$$

1 🧑 has been saving for a holiday. His savings can be represented by:

[ ]

(a)   Shade to show 50% of 🧑 's savings.

[ ]

(b)   Shade to show 20% of 🧑 's savings.

[ ]

(c)   Shade to show 25% of 🧑 's savings.

[ ]

(d)   Shade to show 80% of 🧑 's savings.

[ ]

2 Calculate the discounted price.

(a) 10% discount

£40

(b) 25% discount

£50

(c) 20% discount

£8

3 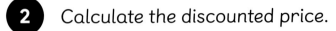 spent 20% of her savings on a gift and 75% of the rest on a book.

savings

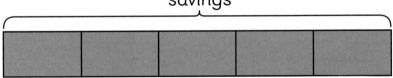

At the end, had £29 left. How much did she have before she bought the gift and the book?

Complete Worksheet **2** – Page **3 - 7**

Finding Percentage Change

In Focus

The number of pupils in a school has been increasing by about 10% each year since 2010. In 2011, the number of pupils was 220.

Let's Learn

1   10% of 220 =

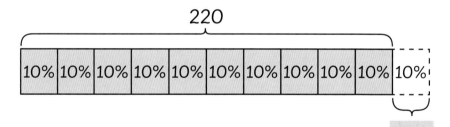

220

10% 10% 10% 10% 10% 10% 10% 10% 10% 10% 10%

10% of 220 =

$220 \div 10 = 22$

In 2012, the number of pupils was 220 + 22 or 242.

2 10% of 242 = [ ]

242

| 10% | 10% | 10% | 10% | 10% | 10% | 10% | 10% | 10% | 10% | 10% |

[ ]

242 ÷ 10 = 24.2 ≈ 24 (to the nearest whole number)

In 2013, the number of pupils was 242 + 24 or 266.

When the number of pupils went up by 24 from 242, that's about a 10% increase.

3 10% of 266 = [ ]

266

| 10% | 10% | 10% | 10% | 10% | 10% | 10% | 10% | 10% | 10% | 10% |

[ ]

266 ÷ 10 = 26.6 ≈ 27 (to the nearest whole number)

In 2014, the number of pupils was 266 + 27 or 293.

4 Calculate the number of pupils in 2010.

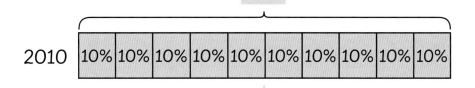

2010 | 10% | 10% | 10% | 10% | 10% | 10% | 10% | 10% | 10% | 10%

2011 | 10% | 10% | 10% | 10% | 10% | 10% | 10% | 10% | 10% | 10% | 10%

220

$220 \div 11 = 20$

$10 \times 20 = 200$

Check.
10% of 200 = 20
200 + 20 = 220

In 2010, the number of pupils was 200.

If the number of pupils continues to increase by 10% each year, in which year do you expect it to reach about 430 pupils?

Guided Practice

1 The price of breakfast at a café has increased by 15%. It used to be £4.50. Find the new price.

2 The price of lunch at a restaurant has increased by 20%. It is now £9.60. Find the old price.

Complete Worksheet **3** – Page **8 - 9**

Using Percentage to Compare

In Focus

 has 50 coins in his collection.

 has 20 more coins than has.

Describe, in different ways, how many more coins has than .

Let's Learn

1 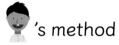's method

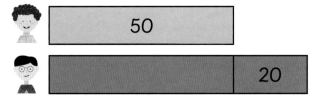

I use a diagram.

2 's method

I say the number of coins.

 has more coins than . 20 more.

3  's method

20%

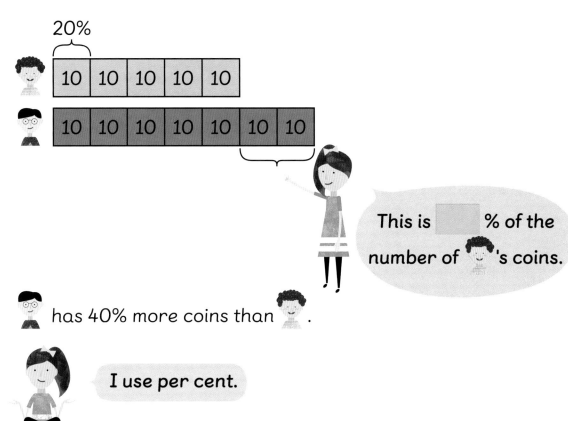

| 10 | 10 | 10 | 10 | 10 |

| 10 | 10 | 10 | 10 | 10 | 10 | 10 |

This is ⬜ % of the number of 's coins.

has 40% more coins than .

I use per cent.

4 's method

Can I say has $\frac{2}{5}$ more coins than has or...

has 0.4 more coins than has?

 You can say has $1\frac{2}{5}$ times as many coins as

or has 1.4 times as many coins as .

1

Class	Number of pupils
6 Red	24
6 Blue	30
6 Green	18

(a) 6 Blue has [   ] % more pupils than 6 Red.

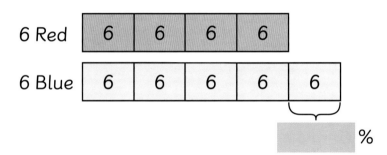

[   ] %

(b) 6 Green has [   ] % fewer pupils than 6 Blue.

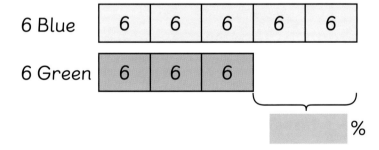

[   ] %

I have £60.

I have 15% less money than .

I have 20% more money than .

(a) How much money does have?

(b) How much money does have?

Complete Worksheet 4 – Page **10 - 11**

Mind Workout

 and had £820 altogether. After spent 30% of his money

and spent 50% of her money, they had £494 left. Find the amount that

 and each had to begin with.

We write £0.20 to show 20 p.

Can we also write it as £ $\frac{1}{5}$ or £20%?

I can say 20% of an amount of money.

Can I also say $\frac{1}{5}$ of an amount of money...

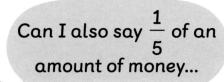

or 0.2 of an amount of money?

Self Check

I know how to...

☐ calculate the percentage of a number and a quantity.

☐ use percentage to describe changes.

☐ use percentage to compare.

Recipe

15 minutes preparation time
12 minutes cooking time
Makes 48 pieces

6 oz (175 g.) self-raising flour
6 oz (175 g.) butter, softened
6 oz (175 g.) caster sugar
5 oz (145 g.) brown sugar
2 eggs
1 tsp vanilla extract
$\frac{3}{4}$ tsp salt
$\frac{3}{4}$ tsp baking soda
6 oz (175 g.) oats
2 oz (60 g.) sunflower seeds
2 oz (60 g.) flax seeds
2 oz (60 g.) millet
2 oz (60 g.) raisins
4 oz (120 g.) chocolate chips

How can we compare the amounts of the various ingredients in this recipe?

Chapter 8
Ratio

Comparing Quantities

In Focus

Compare the number of boys and the number of girls in different ways.

Let's Learn

1

The number of girls is 3 times the number of boys.

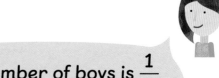

The number of boys is $\frac{1}{3}$ the number of girls.

The number of boys is 25% of the number of children.

The number of boys is $\frac{1}{4}$ the number of children.

2

For each boy, there are 3 girls.

Guided Practice

1 The number of 🍎🍎🍎🍎 is ☐ times the number of 🍎 .

For every 1 🍎 , there are ☐ 🍎 .

2 The number of ⬤⬤⬤⬤⬤⬤⬤⬤⬤⬤⬤⬤⬤⬤⬤ is ☐ times

the number of ⬤⬤⬤ .

For every ☐ ⬤ , there are ☐ ⬤ .

3 The number of ⬤⬤⬤⬤⬤⬤ is ☐ times the number of

⬤⬤⬤⬤⬤⬤⬤⬤⬤⬤⬤⬤⬤⬤⬤⬤⬤⬤ .

For every ☐ ⬤ , there are ☐ ⬤ .

Complete Worksheet 1 – Page 17 – 18

Comparing Quantities

In Focus

For every [   ] 🔲 , there are [   ] ⚫ .

Let's Learn

1

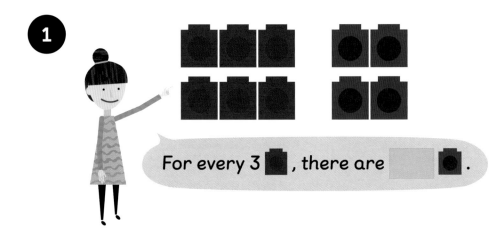

For every 3 🔲 , there are [   ] ⚫ .

2 There are [   ] times as many 🔲 as there are ⚫ .

There are [   ] % more 🔲 than ⚫ .

Guided Practice

1

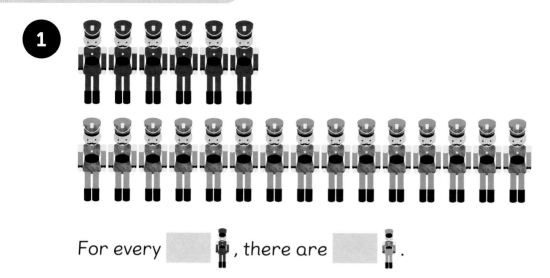

For every ☐ 🪖 , there are ☐ 🪖 .

2

For every ☐ ⬤ , there are ☐ ◐ .

3

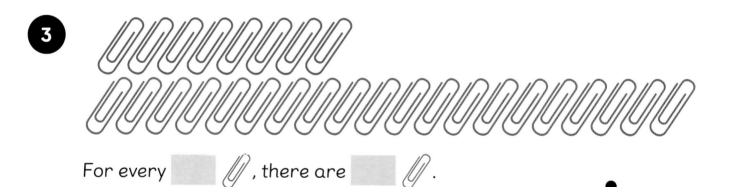

For every ☐ 📎 , there are ☐ 📎 .

Try to compare
the numbers in
other ways.

Complete Worksheet **2** – Page **19 - 20**

Comparing Quantities

Compare the amounts of each ingredient needed to make lemonade.

Lemonade Recipe

6   cold water

2   lemon juice (8-10 lemons)

1   sugar

a pinch of salt

Let's Learn

1   For every 🥤 of sugar, you need [ ] 🥤 of lemon juice.

sugar

lemon juice

2   For every 🥤 of lemon juice, you need [ ] 🥤 of cold water.

lemon juice

cold water

The ratio of the volume of lemon juice to the volume of cold water needed is 1 : 3.

Ratio = 1 : 3

This means that for every 1 cup of lemon juice, 3 cups of cold water are needed.

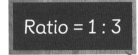

We read 1 : 3 as '1 to 3'.

Guided Practice

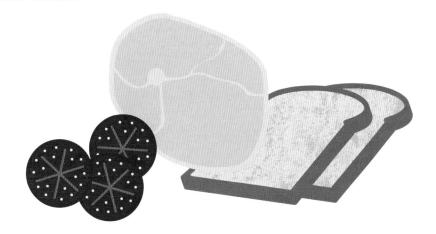

(a)   For every slice of ham, we need [   ] slices of bread.

   The ratio of the number of ham slices to bread slices = [   ] : [   ] .

(b)   For every slice of ham, we need [   ] slices of tomato.

   The ratio of the number of ham slices to tomato slices = [   ] : [   ] .

(c)   For every 2 slices of bread, we need [   ] slices of tomato.

   The ratio of the number of bread slices to tomato slices = [   ] : [   ] .

Complete Worksheet **3** – Page **21 – 22**

Comparing Quantities

In Focus

The shorter piece is $\dfrac{3}{5}$ the length of the longer piece.

The ratio of the lengths is 3 : 5.

Let's Learn

Is this $\dfrac{3}{5}$ the length of the other?

1

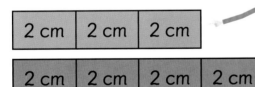

2 cm	2 cm	2 cm

2 cm	2 cm	2 cm	2 cm	2 cm

Ratio = 6 cm : 10 cm

= 3 : 5

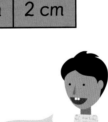

3 to 5

It means for every 3 cm of the green piece, there are 5 cm of the orange piece.

2 The ratio of the length of a shorter strip of paper to the length of a longer strip of paper is 3 : 5.

(a) If the shorter strip is 18 cm, how long is the longer strip?

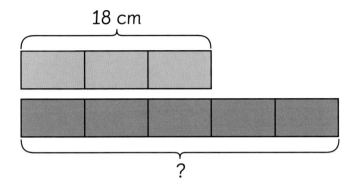

18 ÷ 3 = 6 cm

5 × 6 = 30 cm

The longer strip is 30 cm.

(b) If the longer strip is 18 cm, how long is the shorter strip?

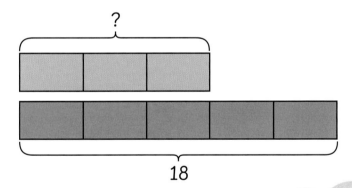

18 ÷ 5 = 3.6 cm

3 × 3.6 = 10.8 cm

The shorter strip is 10.8 cm.

18 ÷ 5 = 36 ÷ 10
= 3.6 cm

3 × 3 = 9 cm
3 × 0.6 = 1.8 cm

Guided Practice

1 Find the ratio.

(a)

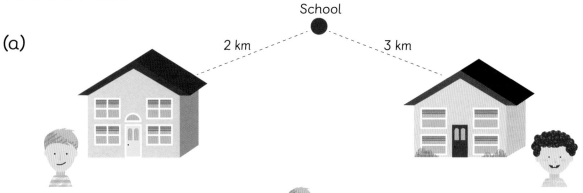

The ratio of the distance of 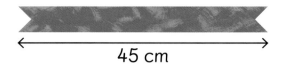's home from school to the distance

of 's home from school is ⬚ : ⬚ .

(b)

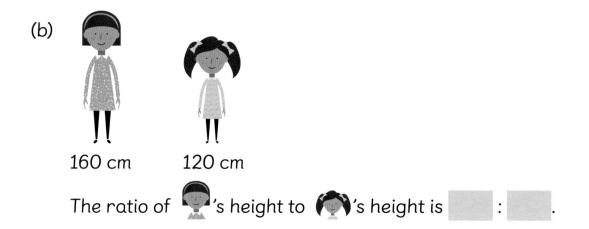

160 cm   120 cm

The ratio of 's height to 's height is ⬚ : ⬚ .

2 This piece of ribbon is cut in two so that the ratio of the length of the longer piece to that of the shorter piece is 5 : 4.

45 cm

How long is the longer piece?

Complete Worksheet **4 – Page 23 – 24** ▶

Comparing Quantities

Compare the average mass of the Asian elephant shown to that of the zebra shown.

2700 kg

450 kg

Let's Learn

1 Ratio = 2700 kg : 450 kg

= ☐ : ☐

| 900 kg | 900 kg | 900 kg |

| 450 kg |

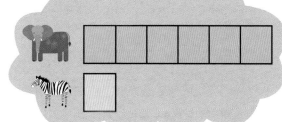

The mass of the  is 6 times the mass of the .

We say the ratio of the 🐘's mass to the 🦓's mass is 6 : 1.

2 The ratio of 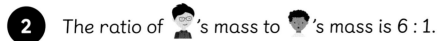's mass to 🧑🏾's mass is 6 : 1.

🧑‍🦱 weighs 72 kg. Find 🧑🏾's mass.

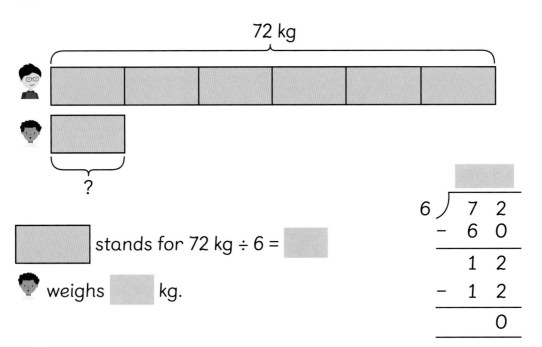

72 kg

?

[   ] stands for 72 kg ÷ 6 = [   ]

🧑🏾 weighs [   ] kg.

```
        [   ]
   6 ) 7 2
     - 6 0
       1 2
     - 1 2
         0
```

Guided Practice

1 A website gives the average mass of some animals.

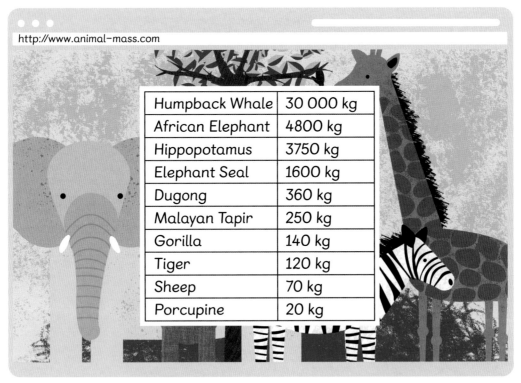

http://www.animal-mass.com

Humpback Whale	30 000 kg
African Elephant	4800 kg
Hippopotamus	3750 kg
Elephant Seal	1600 kg
Dugong	360 kg
Malayan Tapir	250 kg
Gorilla	140 kg
Tiger	120 kg
Sheep	70 kg
Porcupine	20 kg

(a) Find the ratio of the mass of the African elephant to that of the elephant seal.

(b) Find the ratio of the mass of the Malayan tapir to that of the hippopotamus.

(c) Which two animals have masses that are in the following ratios?
 (i) 1 : 2
 (ii) 1 : 3
 (iii) 6 : 7

2 The ratio of the mass of 🧑's pet now to its mass a year ago is 5 : 4.
(a) What does this mean?

Its mass now is 8 kg.
(b) Find its mass a year ago.

now

a year ago

Complete Worksheet **5** – Page **25** – **26**

Comparing Numbers

In Focus

| 12 | 18 |

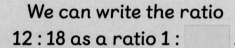

We can write the ratio 12 : 18 as a ratio 1 : ▢ .

You can for other numbers, but not for 12 : 18.

Who is correct?

Let's Learn

1 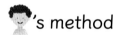's method

| 12 | 2 | 2 | 2 | 2 | 2 | 2 |

| 18 | 2 | 2 | 2 | 2 | 2 | 2 | 2 | 2 | 2 |

12 : 18 = 6 : 9

2 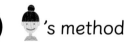's method

| 12 | 3 | 3 | 3 | 3 |

| 18 | 3 | 3 | 3 | 3 | 3 | 3 |

12 : 18 = 4 : 6

3 's method

12 | 6 | 6 |

18 | 6 | 6 | 6 |

The ratio of 12 to 18 is 2 : 3.

This is the ratio in its simplest form.

12 : 18 = 2 : 3

4 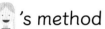's method

12 | 12 |

18 | 12 | 6 |

12 : 18 cannot be written as a ratio 1 : ⬜ .

Guided Practice

1 Write the ratio of the numbers in the simplest form.

(a) 10 : 5

(b) 8 : 6

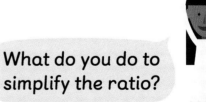

What do you do to simplify the ratio?

(c) 36 : 81

(d) 48 : 144

2 (a) The ratio of one number to another is 3 : 4. Their sum is 168. Find the numbers.

(b) The ratio of one number to another is 7 : 4. Their difference is 168. Find the numbers.

Complete Worksheet 6 – Page **27 - 28**

Solving Word Problems

In Focus

The ratio of 's savings to 's savings is 1 : 3. Their total savings are £2448.

Can you work out what each of them has saved?

Let's Learn

1 Use guess-and-check.

		total

2 Use a model.

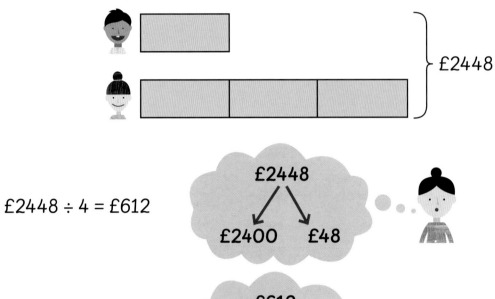

$£2448 \div 4 = £612$

$£612 \times 3 = £1836$

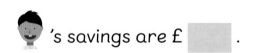 stands for £612.

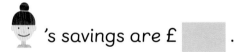 's savings are £ [ ] .

's savings are £ [ ] .

Which method do you prefer: guess-and-check or calculation?

Guided Practice

1  and  share £18 in the ratio of 1 : 2.  receives the larger part. How much does  receive?

2

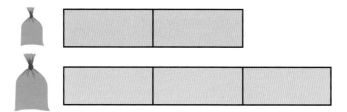

The bag of flour is separated into two portions. The ratio of the mass of the lighter portion to that of the heavier portion is 2 : 3. What is the mass of the heavier portion?

3 The ratio of 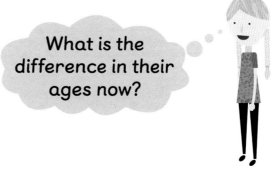's age to his father's age is 3 : 10. His father was 28 years old when was born. How old is now?

What is the difference in their ages now?

Complete Worksheet **7** – Page **29 – 30**

Solving Word Problems

In Focus

The ratio of the number of  to the number of 🧁 is 2 : 3. There are 36 more 🧁 than 🧁. There are 372 cupcakes in all. Is it possible to find the number of each type of cupcake?

Let's Learn

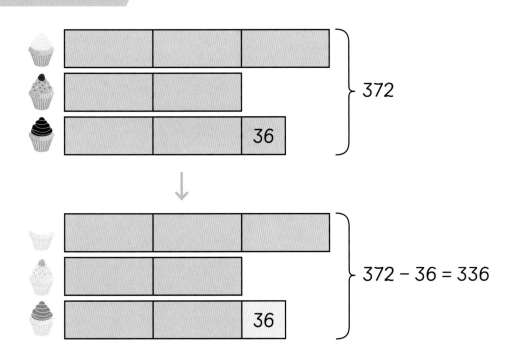

🧁 ⟩ 372

🧁 ⟩ 372 − 36 = 336

36

⬜ stands for 336 ÷ 7 = 48.

🧁 3 × 48 = ⬜

🧁 2 × 48 = ⬜

🧁 2 × 48 + 36 = ⬜

```
      ⬜
7 ) 3 3 6
  − 2 8 0
    ───────
        5 6
      − 5 6
      ───────
          0
```

Guided Practice

1 baked three types of cookies.

The ratio of the number of to the number of is 3 : 1. The ratio of the number of to the number of is 2 : 1. She baked 180 cookies in all. Find the number of she baked.

2 prepared three types of sandwiches.

The ratio of the number of to the number of is 3 : 1. The ratio of the number of to the number of is 2 : 1. He prepared 180 sandwiches in all. Find the number of he prepared.

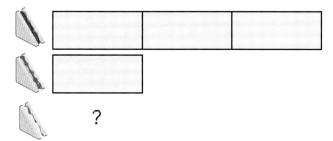

3   made jellies in three different shapes.

The ratio of the number of to the number of ⬤ is 4 : 3.

There are 10 more ▢ than ⬤ . She made 180 jellies in all.

Find the number of ▢ she made.

⭐ | _ | _ | _ | _ |

⬤   ?

▢   ?

4 made three types of lollies.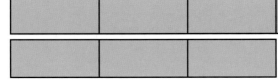

The ratio of the number of  to the number of  is 4 : 3. There are

10 fewer 🍡 than 🍫 . She made 180 lollies in all. Find the number of

🍡 she made.

🍦 | _ | _ | _ | _ |

🍫 | _ | _ | _ |

🍡   ?

Complete Worksheet **8** – Page **31 - 34**

Solving Word Problems

In Focus

The ratio of the number of 😊 's coins to those of 👤 was 3 : 1. After 👤 gave 👤 33 coins and 👤 received another 12 coins from her mother, 😊 still had 4 more coins than 👤 . Is this possible?

Let's Learn

1

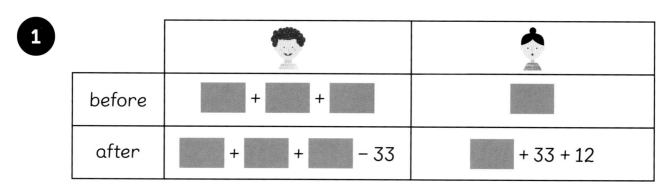

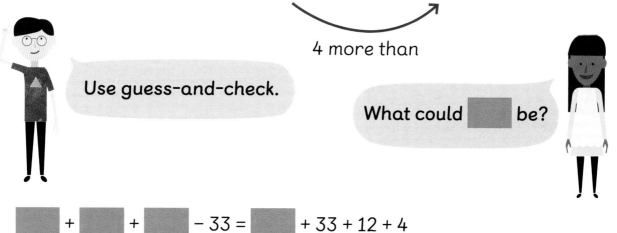

Use guess-and-check.

What could ▢ be?

4 more than

▢ + ▢ + ▢ − 33 = ▢ + 33 + 12 + 4

2 Use a model.

before

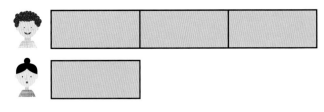

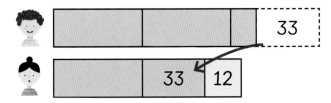

after

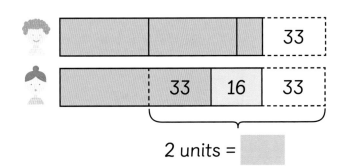

33

33 | 12

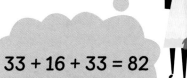

33

33 | 16 | 33

2 units = ▢

12 + 4 = 16

33 + 16 + 33 = 82

2 units = 82

1 unit = 82 ÷ 2

= 41

 had 3 × 41 = 123 coins at first.

 had 41 coins at first.

Guided Practice

1 The ratio of the number of boys to the number of girls at a camp was 4 : 1. After 21 girls went home, there were 8 times as many boys as girls. How many children were at the camp before the 21 girls went home?

before   boys

girls

2 The ratio of the number of children playing football to those playing basketball was 4 : 1. After 21 children changed from playing football to basketball, the ratio became 1 : 2.

How many children were playing football before the 21 children changed games?

before

Complete Worksheet 9 – Page 35 – 37 ▶

Mind Workout ▶

 had some and .

The ratio of the value of the coins to the value of the notes was 1 : 2. After

spending an equal number of coins and notes, the ratio of the number of coins

to the number of notes became 2 : 1.

How much money could have at first? Are there other solutions?

Maths Journal

There are almost 300 flights each day between the Brazilian cities of Rio de Janeiro and Sao Paulo.

The Australian cities of Melbourne and Sydney are also very well connected. The ratio of the number of daily flights between the Brazilian cities to the number of daily flights between the Australian cities is 3 : 2.

Describe the information about the number of flights linking the two pairs of cities in other ways without using ratio.

For every 3 flights between the Brazilian cities, there are 2 flights between the Australian cities.

Try to use the word 'times'.

Try to use fractions or percentages.

I know how to...

☐ compare quantities and numbers using ratios.

☐ solve problems involving ratios.

Self Check

Do you know how algebra is used?

Al-jabr
Muhammad
830

5

x
3

x + 2x + 3x = 12

Chapter 9
Algebra

Describing a Pattern

In Focus

 arranges coins according to a rule.

What is the rule?

Let's Learn

Pattern number	1	2	3	4	5
Arrangement					

Can you show Pattern 6?

In Pattern 6, there are 6 rows.

The longest row in Pattern 6 has 6 coins.

2 How about Pattern 10?

In Pattern 10, there are ▢ rows.

The longest row in Pattern 10 has ▢ coins.

3 How about Pattern Δ where Δ is any whole number?

Pattern number	Number of rows	Number of coins in the longest row
1	1	1
2	2	2
3	3	3
4	4	4
5	5	5
6	6	6
10	10	10
Δ	Δ	

4 We can use a symbol (Δ) or a letter (x) to stand for any number.

In Pattern x, there are ▢ rows.

The longest row in Pattern x has ▢ coins.

Work in pairs.

① Make a pattern using the pattern blocks according to a rule.

What you need:

② Your partner will guess the rule that you use and show the next pattern.

③ Switch roles and repeat ① and ②.

Guided Practice

 makes this pattern according to a rule.

Pattern number	1	2	3	4
Arrangement				

Complete the table.

Pattern number	Number of ■	Number of ▲
1		
2		
3		
4		
10		
n		

Complete Worksheet 1 – Page 43 – 44 ▶

Describing a Pattern

In Focus

 makes rectangles according to a rule.

Rectangle 1   Rectangle 2   Rectangle 3

What is the rule?

Let's Learn

1 Make Rectangle 4 and Rectangle 5.

Rectangle number	1	2	3	4	5

2 Complete the table.

How is the rectangle number related to the length of its sides?

Rectangle number	Length of shorter side	Length of longer side
1	1 unit	2 units
2	2 units	3 units
3	3 units	4 units
4	4 units	5 units
5	5 units	6 units
10	___ units	___ units

3 Describe Rectangle 99 and Rectangle m.

The length of the shorter side is the same as the rectangle number.

m stands for any whole number.

The length of the longer side is 1 more than the rectangle number.

Rectangle number	Length of shorter side (units)	Length of longer side (units)
99	99	99 + 1 = 100
m	m	$m + 1$

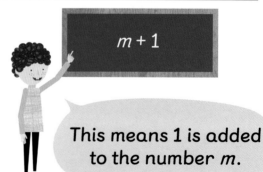

$m + 1$

This means 1 is added to the number m.

1, 2, 3 are consecutive whole numbers. So are 3, 4, 5 and 10, 11, 12, 13.

1 x, ▢ and ◣ are consecutive whole numbers.

(a) Write ▢ in terms of x.

(b) Write ◣ in terms of x.

2 ◉ writes down 10 consecutive whole numbers starting with y.

(a) Write the second number in ◉'s list.

(b) Write the tenth number in ◉'s list.

3 ◉ writes down three consecutive odd numbers.

z, $z + 2$, ▢

(a) Is the second number correctly written? Explain.

(b) Write down the third number on ◉'s list.

Complete Worksheet **2** – Page **45 – 46**

Describing a Pattern

**In Focus**

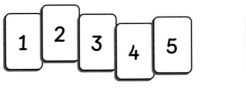

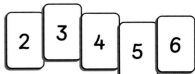

> Arrange the five cards
>
> so that the vertical sum equals the horizontal sum.

> Try using another five consecutive whole numbers.

1, 2, 3, 4, 5 and 7, 8, 9, 10, 11 are consecutive whole numbers.

What do you notice about the arrangements that work?

Let's Learn

1 uses , , , , .

	3	
2	1	5
	4	

sum = 8

	2	
1	3	5
	4	

sum = 9

	2	
1	5	4
	3	

sum = 10

2 + 1 + 5

1 + 3 + 5

2 uses  .

```
    4
3   2   6
    5
```
sum = 11

```
    3
2   4   6
    5
```
sum = 12

```
    3
2   6   5
    4
```
sum = 13

Activity Time

Work in pairs.

① Arrange 5 consecutive numbers in this arrangement:

```
  ▢
▢ ▢ ▢
  ▢
```

What you need:

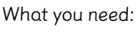
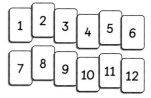

② The sum of should be equal to the sum of ▢▦▢ .

③ What do you notice? Record your observations in a table.

3 Complete these arrangements. Which numbers can go in the middle?

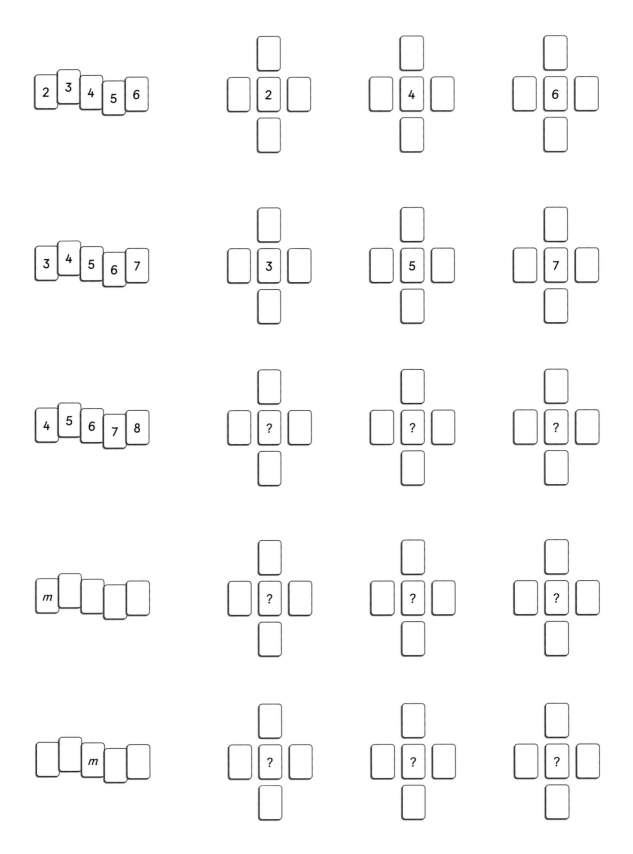

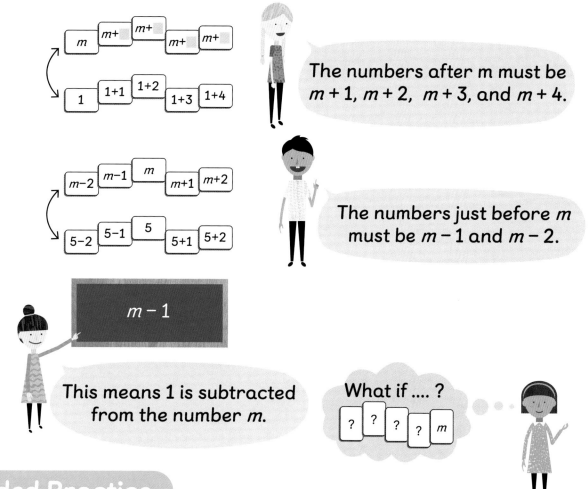

The numbers after m must be m + 1, m + 2, m + 3, and m + 4.

The numbers just before m must be m − 1 and m − 2.

m − 1

This means 1 is subtracted from the number m.

What if .... ?

Guided Practice

1 ☐ , ☐ , ☐ are consecutive whole numbers. Write the missing numbers in terms of a, b or c.

(a) a , ? , ?   (b) ? , b , ?   (c) ? , ? , c

2 ☐ , ☐ , ☐ are consecutive even numbers. Write the missing numbers in terms of x, y or z.

(a) x , ? , ?   (b) ? , y , ?   (c) ? , ? , z

Complete Worksheet **3** – Page **47**

Describing a Pattern

In Focus

Arrange consecutive whole numbers in

so that the sum of is equal to the sum of .

What do you notice about the two equal sums?

Let's Learn

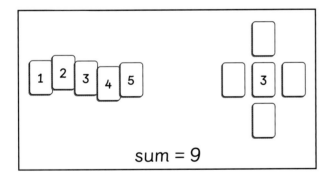

sum = 9

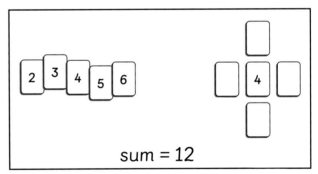

sum = 12

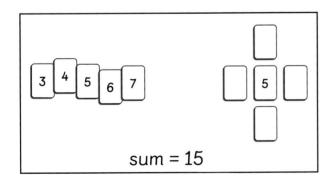

sum = 15

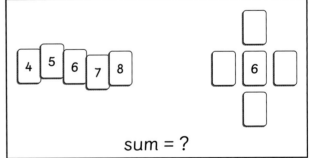

sum = ?

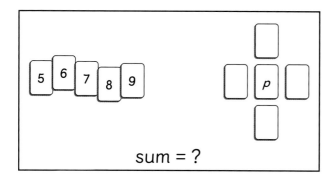

sum = ?

When the middle number goes in the centre, the sum is equal to 3 times as much as.

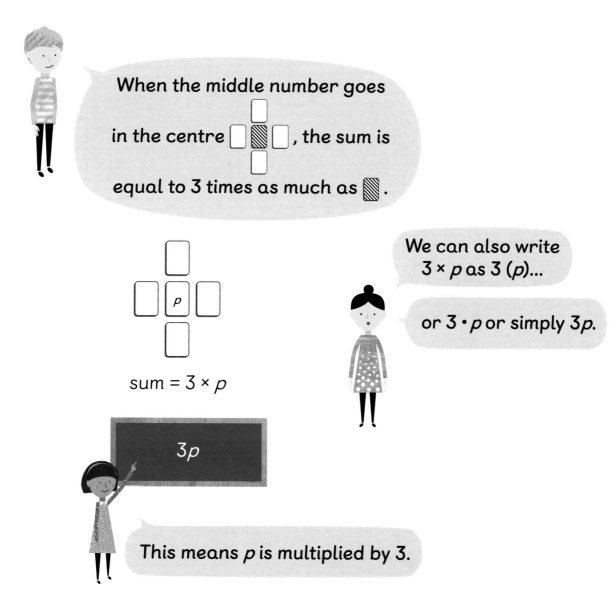

sum = 3 × *p*

We can also write 3 × *p* as 3 (*p*)...

or 3 • *p* or simply 3*p*.

3*p*

This means *p* is multiplied by 3.

3*p* is an **expression**.

1 arranges coins in rectangular arrays. How many coins are there in each arrangement?

Number of rows	1	2	3	4	5	20	n
Number of coins	4	8					

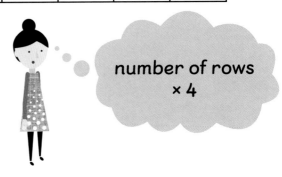

number of rows
× 4

2 thinks of a number. He then multiples it by 3.

x

?

Write an expression for the product.

Complete Worksheet **4 – Page 48**

Writing Algebraic Expressions

In Focus

This number machine changes the input number according to a rule.

Input	5	6	7	8	9	10	99
Output	2	3	4	5	6	?	?

What is the rule?

Let's Learn

1 thinks that the machine halves each input number.

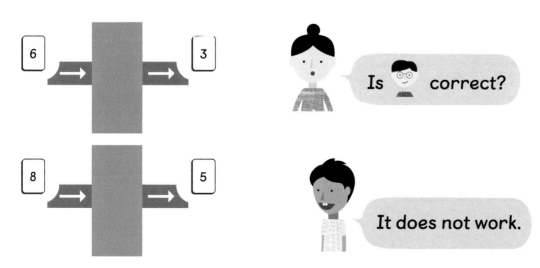

Is correct?

It does not work.

thinks that the machine reduces the number.

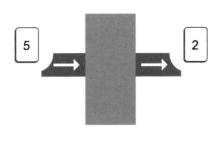

It works! The machine subtracts 3 from each input number.

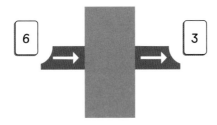

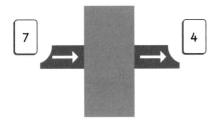

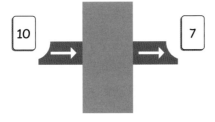

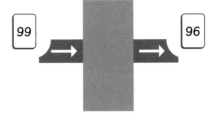

3 What if the number that goes in is ▲ ?

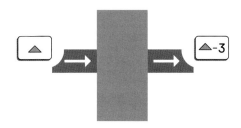

What if the number that goes in is *x*?

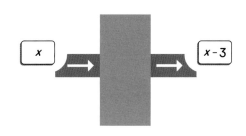

This means the number is 3 less than the number *x*.

x − 3 is an algebraic expression.

Activity Time

Work in pairs.

① Make up a rule.

What you need:

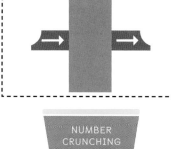

② Show your partner how your machine works. Use three examples to demonstrate.

③ Have your friend guess your rule and use an algebraic expression to describe the rule.

Write an algebraic expression to describe the rule used by each machine.

1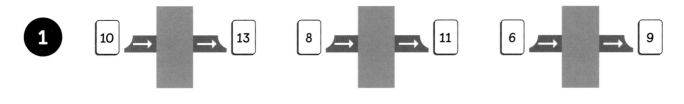

2

3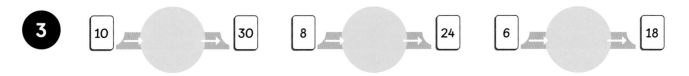

4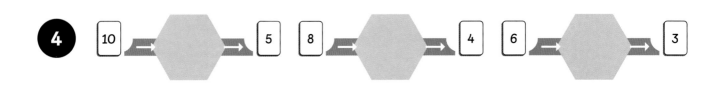

Let the number put in be *y*.

Complete Worksheet **5** – Page **49 – 50**

Writing and Evaluating Algebraic Expressions

In Focus

What could the rule be?

Let's Learn

 1 thinks it is $x - 8$.

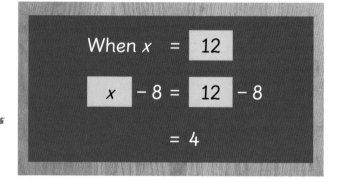

When $x = 12$

$$x - 8 = 12 - 8$$

$$= 4$$

Is correct?

When $x = 12$, $x - 8 = 4$

 2 thinks it is $\frac{1}{3}x$.

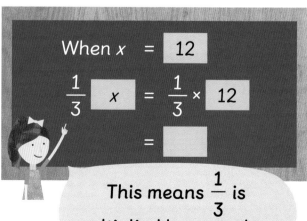

When $x = 12$

$$\frac{1}{3}x = \frac{1}{3} \times 12$$

$$=$$

Is correct?

This means $\frac{1}{3}$ is multiplied by a number.

When $x = 12$, $\frac{1}{3}x = 4$

Algebra   Page 61

3 thinks it is $x \div 3$.

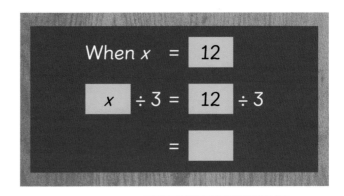

When $x = 12$, $x \div 3 = 4$

We write $x \div 3$ simply as $\dfrac{x}{3}$.

This means the number x divided by 3.

If we use a fraction bar for division, then we do not need the $\div$.

Guided Practice

1 Write an algebraic expression in terms of y to describe the rule used by each machine.

(a)

| 8 | ◯ | 2 | 20 | ◯ | 5 | 12 | ◯ | 3 | y | ◯ | ? |

(b)

| 8 | ▮ | 2 | 20 | ▮ | 14 | 12 | ▮ | 6 | y | ▮ | ? |

2 Complete each table.

(a) $\dfrac{m}{5}$

Input	Output
10	
	10
3	
	3

(b) $n - 5$

Input	Output
10	
	10
	0

Complete Worksheet **6** – Page **51**

Writing and Evaluating Algebraic Expressions

In Focus

makes a pattern using 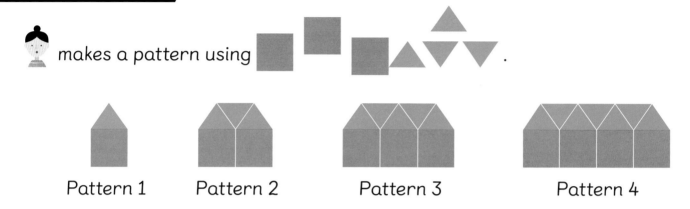.

Pattern 1   Pattern 2   Pattern 3   Pattern 4

How does the number of ⬛ depend on the pattern number?

How does the number of 🔺 depend on the pattern number?

Let's Learn

1 Show Pattern 5 and Pattern 6.

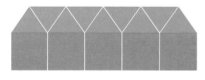   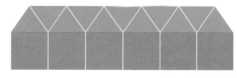

Pattern 5   Pattern 6

2 Complete the table.

Pattern number	■	▲
1	1	1
2	2	3
3	3	5
4	4	
5		
6		
10		
n		

3 Write an expression for the number of ▲ .

The number of ▲ is 1 less than twice the pattern number.

Pattern 1: number of ▲ = 2 × 1 – 1

Pattern 2: number of ▲ = 2 × 2 – 1

Pattern 5: number of ▲ = 2 × 5 – 1

Pattern n: number of ▲ = 2 × n – 1

$2n - 1$

We write it this way.

4 Evaluate $2n - 1$ when $n = 3$.

To **evaluate** means to find the value of.

$$2n - 1 = 2 \times 3 - 1$$
$$= 6 - 1$$
$$= 5$$

Sticks of length 1 are used to make these patterns according to a rule.

Pattern 1   Pattern 2   Pattern 3   Pattern 4

1 Explain why the rule used can be written as:

number of sticks = 3n + 1 where n = pattern number

2 Evaluate 3n + 1 for different values of n.

n	3n + 1
1	
2	3 × 2 + 1 = 7
3	
10	31
99	

when n = 2, 3n + 1 = 7

Complete Worksheet 7 – Page 52 – 54

Writing Formulae

In Focus

4,	7,	10,	13,	16,	...
1st	2nd	3rd	4th	5th	

What is the 99th number in this number pattern?

Continue the pattern.

Let's Learn

1 's method

1st	2nd	3rd	4th	5th	6th	7th
4,	7,	10,	13,	16,	19,	22,

+ 3   + 3   + 3   + 3   + 3   + 3

How can I find the 99th number?

2 's method

1st	2nd	3rd	4th	5th	6th	7th		99th
4	7	10	13	16	19	22	...	?
1 + 3	1 + 6	1 + 9	1 + 12	1 + 15	1 + 18	1 + 21		1 +

1 × 3

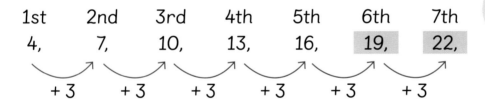

2 × 3

1 + 99 × 3

3 's method

Let p stand for the nth number in the pattern.

$$p = 1 + 3n$$

This says that when $n = 2$, the 2nd number in the pattern is $1 + 3 \times 2 = 7$.

When $n = 6$, 6th number is $p = 1 + 3 \times 6 = 19$

When $n = 7$, 7th number is $p = 1 + 3 \times 7 = 22$

$p = 1 + 3n$ is a formula.

Guided Practice

1 Write a formula for the nth number in each pattern.

I will use T to stand for the nth number in a pattern.

(a)   4, 7, 10, 13, 16, ...

The formula is $T = 1 + 3n$.

(b)   2, 4, 6, 8, 10, ...

(c)   3, 5, 7, 9, 11, ...

(d)   5, 8, 11, 14, 17, ...

2 The formula to find the nth odd number is:

$$n\text{th odd number } x = 2n - 1$$
$$n = 1, \text{ 1st odd number } x = 2 \times 1 - 1 = 1$$
$$n = 2, \text{ 2nd odd number } x = 2 \times 2 - 1 = 3$$

(a)   Find the 5th odd number.

(b)   Find the 99th odd number.

(c)   Find the sum of the first 10 odd numbers.

Complete Worksheet 8 – Page 55 – 56 ▶

Using Formulae

 has this formula for the cooking time of stuffed turkey lighter than 16 lbs.

$t = 90 + 15w$

where t is the cooking time (in minutes) for a turkey of weight w (in lbs).

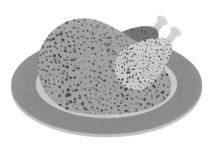

lb is the symbol for pound, a unit of weight.

For turkeys over 16 lbs, the formula is:

$t = 330 + 7.5 (w - 16)$

 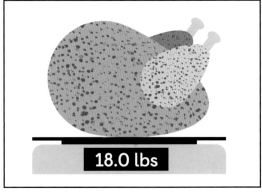

18.0 lbs

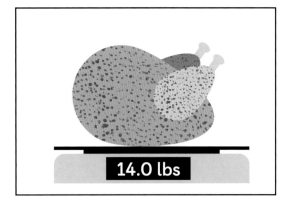 

14.0 lbs

For a dinner party starting at 7 p.m., what is the latest time and should start roasting their stuffed turkey?

1   has a turkey lighter than 16 lbs.

$t = 90 + 15w$

 15*w* means multiply 15 by *w*, where *w* lbs is the weight of the turkey.

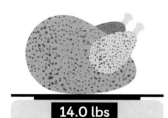

14.0 lbs

$$w = 14, \; t = 90 + 15 \times 14$$
$$= 90 + 210$$
$$= 300$$

300 min = ⬜ h ⬜ min

 should start at ⬜ at the latest.

```
        1  5
  ×     1  4
  ─────────────
        6  0
  +  1  5  0
  ─────────────
     2  1  0
  ─────────────
```

2 has a turkey heavier than 16 lbs.

$t = 330 + 7.5\,(w - 16)$

w − 16 means subtract 16 from *w*, where *w* lbs is the weight of the turkey.

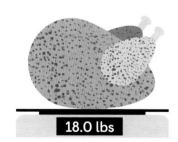

18.0 lbs

$$w = 18, \; t = 330 + 7.5\,(18 - 16)$$
$$= 330 + 7.5\,(2)$$
$$= 330 + 15$$
$$= 345$$

345 min = ⬜ h ⬜ min

 should start at ⬜ at the latest.

The length of the longer side of a rectangle is m cm. The longer side of the rectangle is 1.5 cm greater than the shorter side. The formula to calculate the perimeter p cm is then:

$$p = 4m - 3$$

(a)   Calculate p when $m = 5$.

(b)   Calculate p when the longer side is 10 cm.

(c)   Calculate the lengths of the sides of the rectangle if the perimeter is:

   (i)   31 cm

   (ii)   30 cm

Does this formula work for all rectangles?

Complete Worksheet 9 – Page 57 – 58

Solving Equations

In Focus

The sum of two whole numbers is 9.

Is it possible to find the two numbers?

Yes, if you know one of the numbers.

Yes, even if you do not know one of the numbers.

Who do you agree with?

Let's Learn

1 Write an equation to show the situation.

 + = 9

This is an **equation**.

Use letters to represent the numbers.

Can we use the same letter for both numbers? Are they both the same?

A $x + y = 9$

B $x + x = 9$

Which is correct?

2 What if we know that $x = 3$?

$$x + y = 9$$

$3 +$ ☐ $= 9$ $3 + y = 9$

What value of y makes $3 + y = 9$?

3 What if we are told neither the two values?

$x + y = 9$

x	y	$x + y = 9$
0	9	9
1	8	9
2	7	9
3	6	9
...	...	

How many possible pairs of x and y are there for $x + y = 9$?

1 Find the value of x.

(a) x + 7 = 10

10

| x | 7 |

☐ + 7 = 10

(b) x − 7 = 10

x

| | 7 |

☐ − 7 = 10

(c) 3x = 12

12

| x | x | x |

3 × ☐ = 12

(d) $\frac{x}{3}$ = 12

☐ ÷ 3 = 12

x

| | | |

2 x and y are whole numbers. Find all possible values of x and y.

(a) x + y = 3

(b) x + y = 2

(c) x + y = 5

Do you notice a pattern?

Complete Worksheet **10** – Page **59 – 60**

$$\frac{1}{x} + \frac{1}{y} = \frac{7}{12}$$

x and y are whole numbers. Find the values of x and y.

Maths Journal

 has three times as much money as has. Together they have £12.

Here is how , and 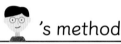 try to work out how much has.

 's method   's method   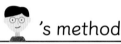 's method

$12 \div 3 = \blacksquare$

$x + 3x = 12$

$\}$ 12

Which methods are correct? Explain why.

I know how to...

☐ describe and complete a pattern.

☐ write and evaluate algebraic expressions.

☐ write and use formulae.

☐ solve equations.

Self Check

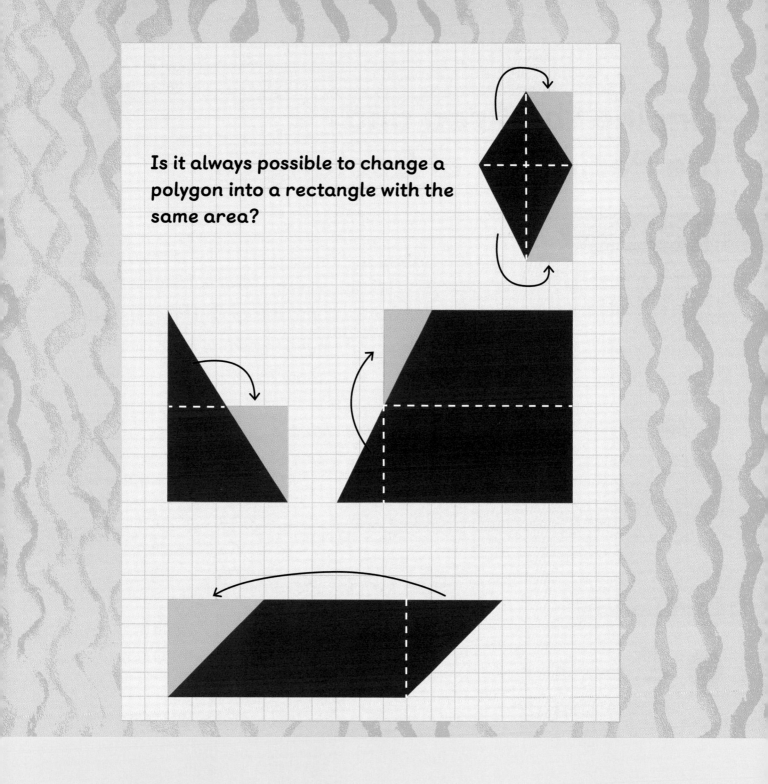

Is it always possible to change a polygon into a rectangle with the same area?

Chapter 10
Area and Perimeter

Finding the Area and the Perimeter of Rectangles

In Focus

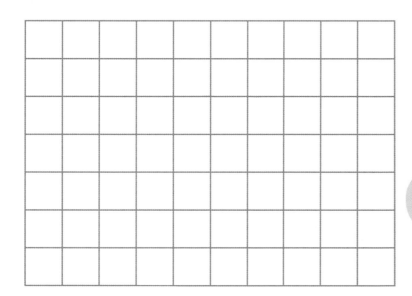

Draw a few rectangles that fit onto this grid. They must either have the same area or the same perimeter.

For each rectangle, use A cm² for the area, and l cm and b cm for the lengths of the sides.

Use p cm for the perimeter of each rectangle.

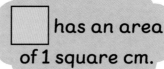

Let's Learn

1 draws this.

area = A cm² = 4 cm²
length = l cm = 4 cm
breadth = b cm = 1 cm

perimeter = p cm
= 10 cm

☐ has an area of 1 square cm.

1 cm²

2 draws a different rectangle with p = 10.

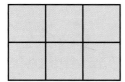

area = A cm² = 6 cm²   perimeter = p cm = 10 cm

length = l cm = 3 cm

breadth = b cm = 2 cm

3 draws this.

area = A cm² = 4 cm²   perimeter = p cm = 8 cm

length = l cm = 2 cm

breadth = b cm = 2 cm

4 draws a different rectangle with p = 8 cm.

area = A cm² = 3 cm²   perimeter = p cm = 8

length = l cm = 3 cm

breadth = b cm = 1 cm

What do you notice about the area and the perimeter of rectangles?

5

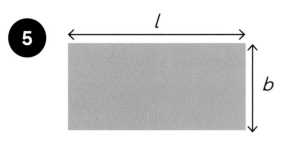

$$A = l \times b$$

This is also written as $A = lb$.

$$p = 2l + 2b$$

$2l$ means twice the value of l.

$2b$ means $2 \times b$.

These are formulas (or formulae).

Guided Practice

1 Find the area of each rectangle.

(a)

4 cm

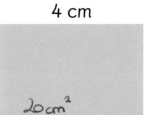

20 cm²

5 cm

(b)

$3\frac{1}{2}$ cm

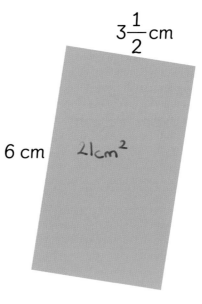

6 cm   21 cm²

2 Show that the area of the rectangle is 32.5 cm².

6.5 cm

Area² = Length × height

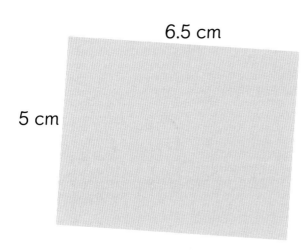

5 cm

²6·5cm
× 5 cm
32· 5

Explain what it means.

3 A rectangle has an area of 20 cm². Its longer side is 8 cm.

(a) Find the length of the other side.

(b) Calculate its perimeter.

$$\begin{array}{r} 02.50 \\ 8\overline{)20.00} \end{array}$$

2·50cm

8cm   8cm

2·50cm

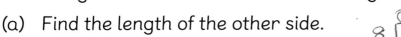

2·5 + 2·5 = 5   5 + 16 = [21]
8 + 8   = 16

4 A square has an area of 25 cm². Find its perimeter.

5
5 [25] 5   Area – 25cm²
5   Perimeter – 20cm

5 A rectangle has an area of 35 cm². Its longer side is ⟨2⟩ cm longer than the other side. Find its perimeter.

Factors of 35   7 – 5 = ②

1 and 35

5 and 7

5
7 [ ] 7   Perimeter : 24.
5

Complete Worksheet **1** – Page **67 – 68**

Finding the Area of Parallelograms

In Focus

A quadrilateral in which each pair of opposite sides is parallel is called a parallelogram.

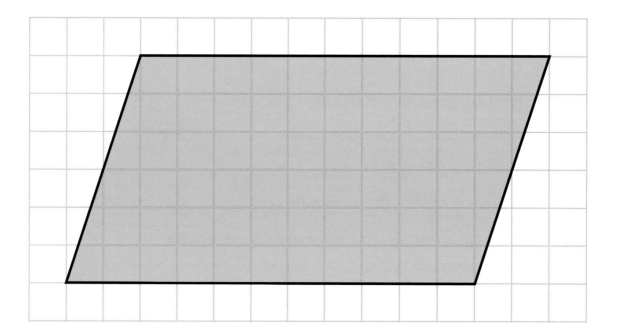

What measurements are needed to find the area of a parallelogram?

Is a rectangle a parallelogram?

Let's Learn

1 did this.

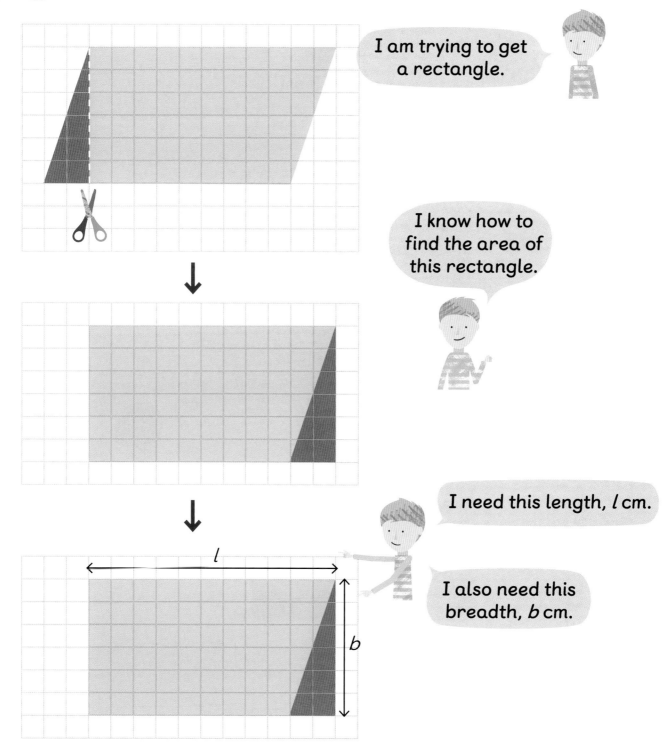

I am trying to get a rectangle.

I know how to find the area of this rectangle.

I need this length, *l* cm.

I also need this breadth, *b* cm.

The area of the parallelogram is equal to the area of the rectangle.

2 Calculate the area of this parallelogram.

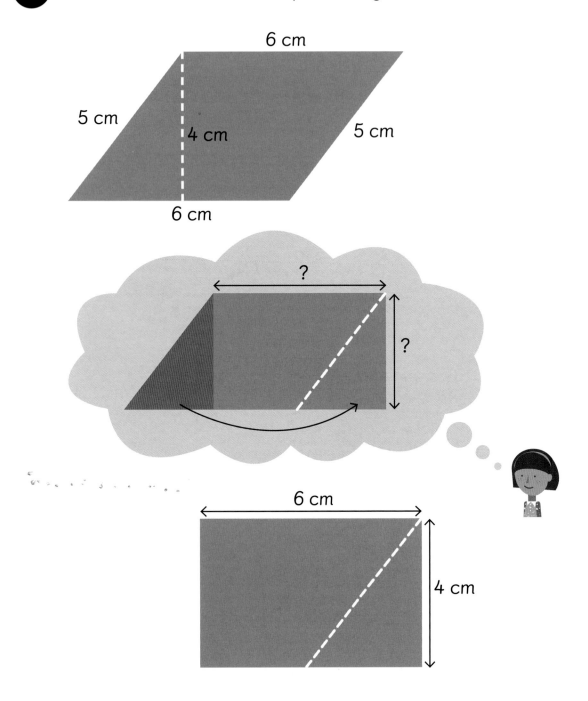

Area of parallelogram = area of rectangle

= (6×4) cm²

= 24 cm²

For rectangles, $A = l \times b$.

Guided Practice

1 Find the area of this parallelogram.

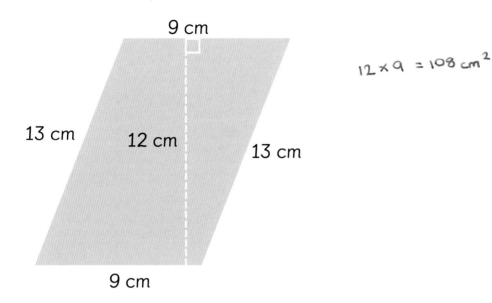

9 cm

13 cm 12 cm 13 cm

9 cm

$12 \times 9 = 108 \text{ cm}^2$

2 Find the area of this parallelogram.

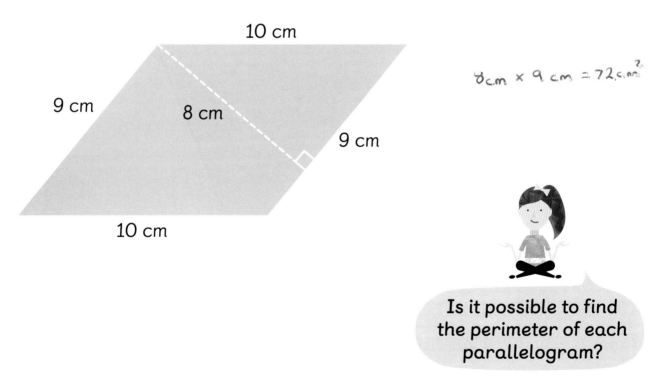

10 cm

9 cm 8 cm 9 cm

10 cm

$8 \text{cm} \times 9 \text{ cm} = 72 \text{ cm}^2$

Is it possible to find the perimeter of each parallelogram?

Complete Worksheet 2 – Page 69

Finding the Area of Triangles

In Focus

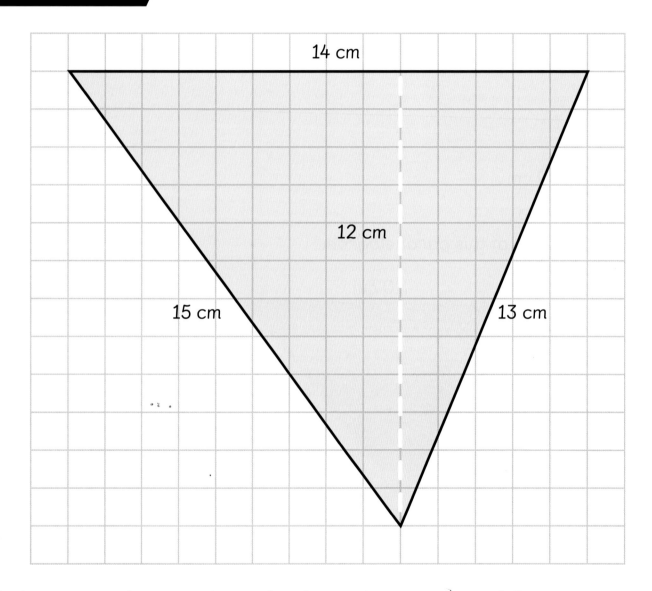

Is there a way this triangle can be changed into a rectangle?

Let's Learn

1 's method

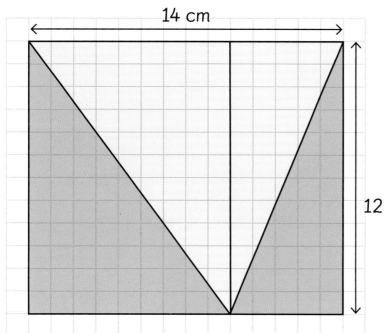

14 cm

12 cm

Area of triangle

$$= \left(\frac{1}{2} \times 14 \times 12\right) \text{ cm}^2$$

$$= \boxed{84} \text{ cm}^2$$

2 's method

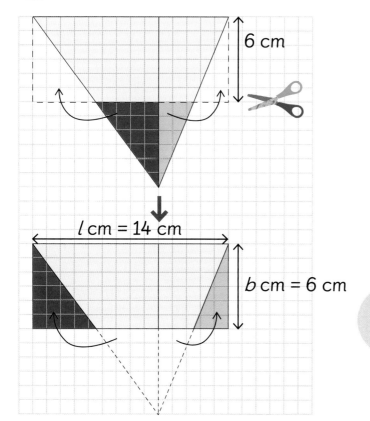

6 cm

l cm = 14 cm

b cm = 6 cm

Area of triangle

$= $ area of rectangle

$$= \left[14 \times \left(\frac{1}{2} \times 12\right)\right] \text{ cm}^2$$

$$= \boxed{84} \text{ cm}^2$$

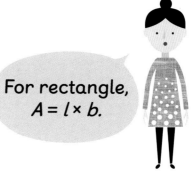

For rectangle,
$A = l \times b.$

Guided Practice

Find the area of the coloured triangles.

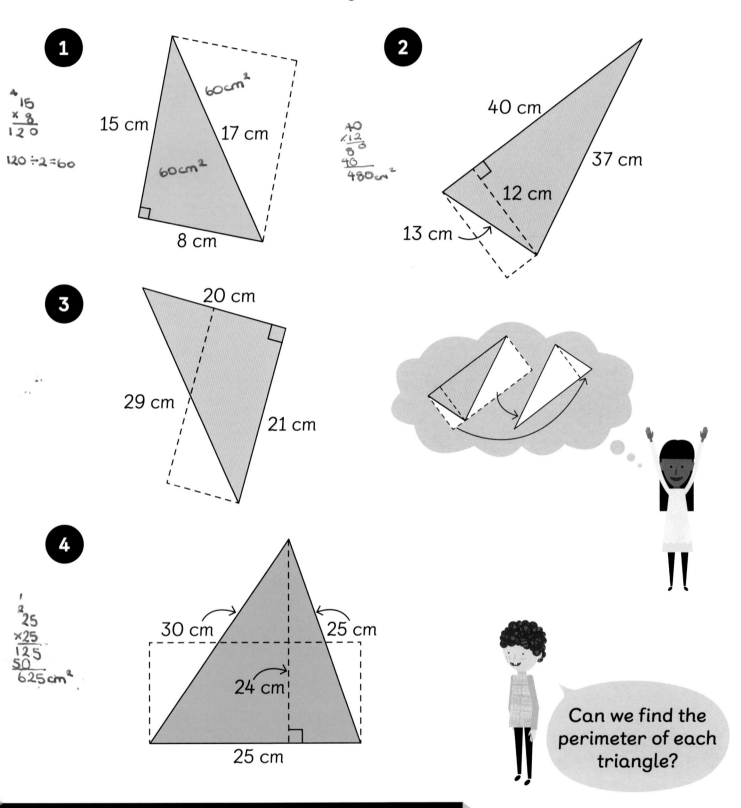

1

15 cm   60 cm²   17 cm

60 cm²

8 cm

15
× 8
120

120 ÷ 2 = 60

2

40 cm   37 cm

12 cm

13 cm

40
×12
8
40
480 cm²

3

20 cm

29 cm   21 cm

4

30 cm   25 cm

24 cm

25 cm

25
×25
125
50
625 cm²

Can we find the perimeter of each triangle?

Complete Worksheet **3** – Page **70 - 71**

Finding the Area of Triangles

In Focus

Draw a triangle.

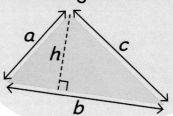

Let a, b, c and h be the lengths shown.

The base is b cm, the height is h cm and the area is A cm².

Show that $A = \frac{1}{2}\,bh$.

Let's Learn

1 's method

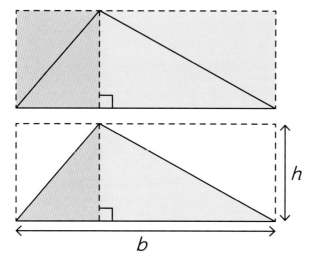

Area of triangle $= \frac{1}{2} \times$ area of rectangle

$A = \frac{1}{2} \times b \times h$

$A = \frac{1}{2}\,bh$

The area of the triangle is half the area of the large rectangle.

area of rectangle $= (b \times h)$ cm²

In algebra, we omit × and write $\frac{1}{2} \times b \times h$ as $\frac{1}{2}bh$.

2 's method

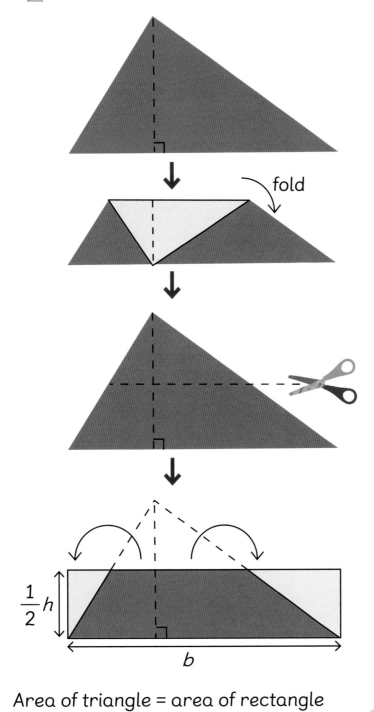

fold

Area of triangle = area of rectangle

$$A = \frac{1}{2} h \times b$$

$$A = \frac{1}{2} hb$$

The area of the pink triangle is equal to the area of the rectangle.

What's the difference between 's method and 's method?

Guided Practice

1 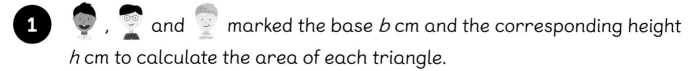 and marked the base *b* cm and the corresponding height *h* cm to calculate the area of each triangle.

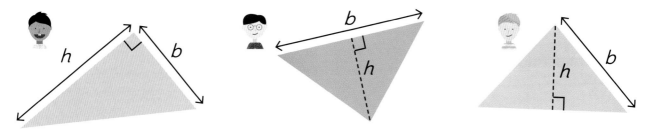

Did they all mark correctly?

Who marked incorrectly? What should he have done?

2 Find the area of each triangle.

(a)

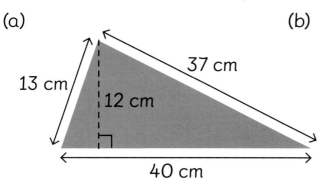

13 cm

37 cm

12 cm

40 cm

(b)

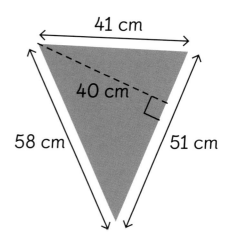

41 cm

40 cm

58 cm

51 cm

3

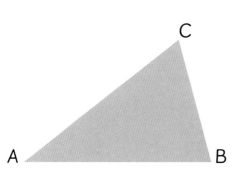

C

A   B

By making the necessary measurements, find the area of triangle ABC.

Complete Worksheet 4 – Page 72 - 73 ▶

Finding the Area of Triangles

In Focus

If the value of *b* is known, what other measurements are needed to find the area of this triangle?

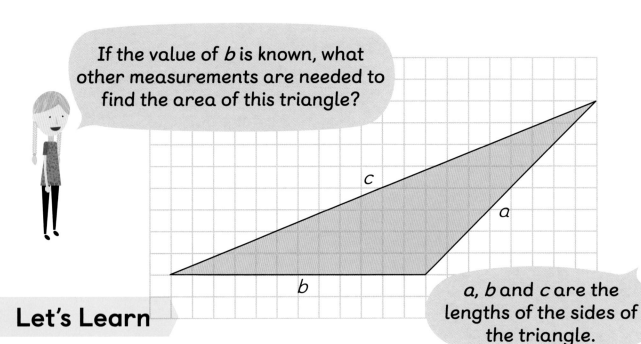

a, *b* and *c* are the lengths of the sides of the triangle.

Let's Learn

1 's method

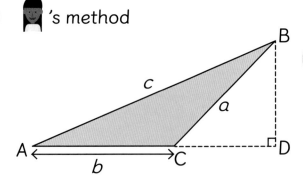

Let's label the vertices with A opposite side *a*, etc.

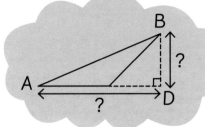

Area of triangle ADB = ▢

Area of triangle CDB = ⬤

Area of triangle ACB = ▢ − ⬤

thinks that she needs the values of x and h.

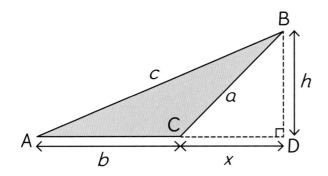

What do you think?

2 's method

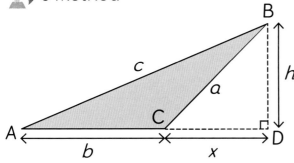

Area of triangle ADB = $\frac{1}{2}(b + x)h$

$\qquad\qquad\qquad\quad = \frac{1}{2}bh + \frac{1}{2}xh$

Area of triangle CDB = $\frac{1}{2}xh$

Area of triangle ACB = area of triangle ADB − area of triangle CDB

$\qquad\qquad\qquad\quad = (\frac{1}{2}bh + \frac{1}{2}xh) - \frac{1}{2}xh$

$\qquad\qquad\qquad\quad = \frac{1}{2}bh$

I need the value of h.

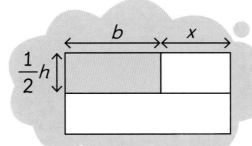

The diagram explains this.

3 's method

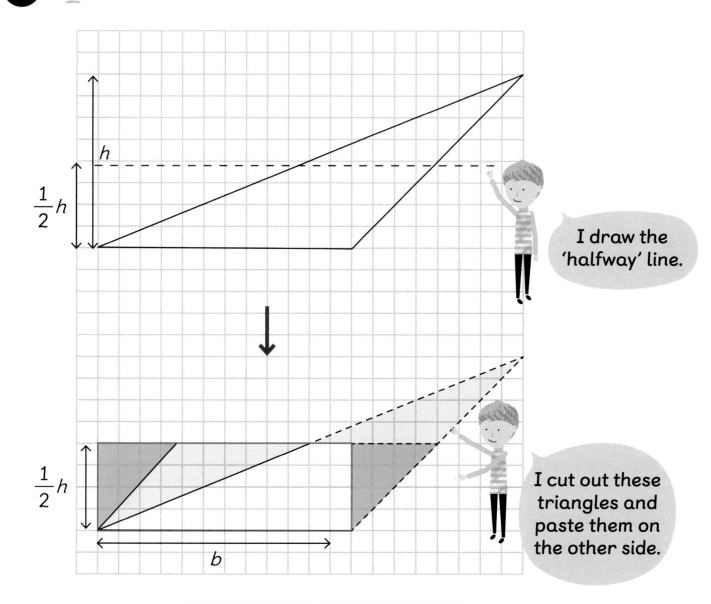

I draw the 'halfway' line.

I cut out these triangles and paste them on the other side.

Is it true that the area of the triangle is the same as the rectangle with lengths of $\frac{1}{2}h$ and b?

 needs the value of h.

Guided Practice

Make the necessary measurements and find the area of each triangle.

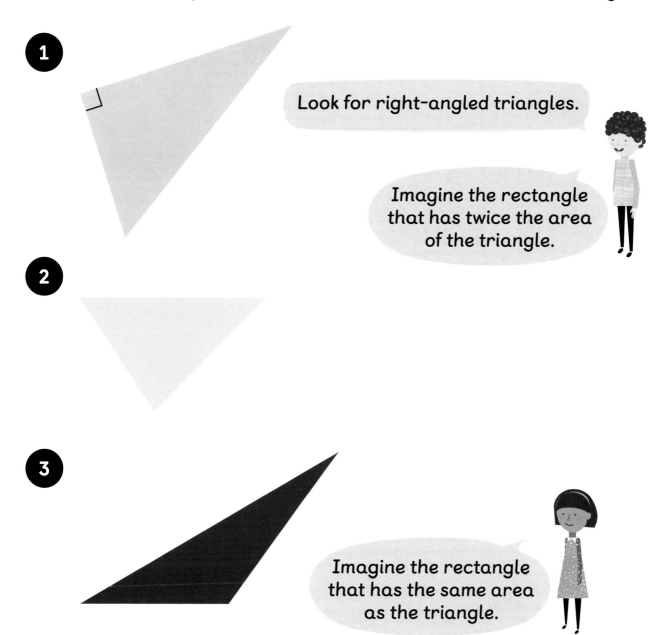

1

Look for right-angled triangles.

Imagine the rectangle that has twice the area of the triangle.

2

3

Imagine the rectangle that has the same area as the triangle.

Complete Worksheet **5** – Page **74 – 76**

Finding the Area of Parallelograms

In Focus

Draw a parallelogram on this grid.

Is it always possible to cut it into two triangles with the same area?

Let's Learn

1  did this.

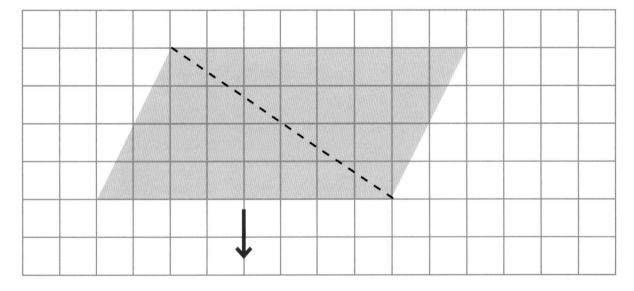

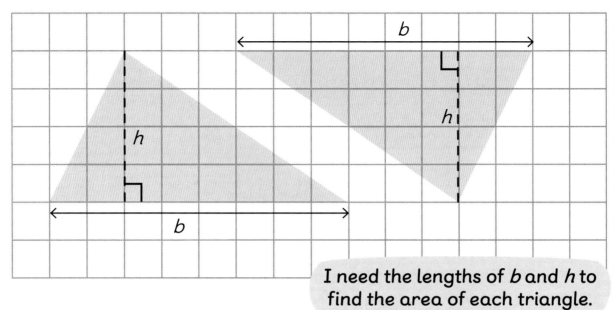

I need the lengths of *b* and *h* to find the area of each triangle.

Area of parallelogram = 2 × area of triangle

Area of parallelogram = *bh*

$\frac{1}{2}$ *bh*

2 did this.

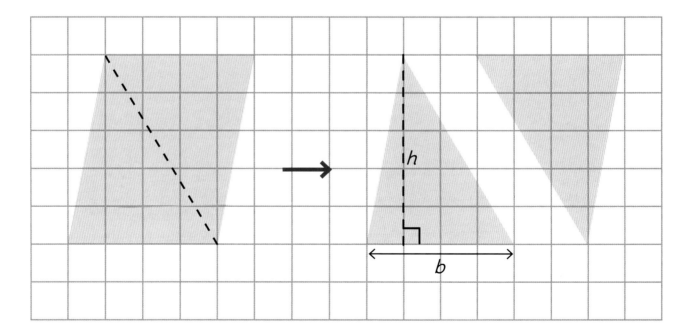

Area of triangle = $\frac{1}{2}$ *bh*

Area of parallelogram = *bh*

Guided Practice

1 By making the necessary measurements, find the area of each parallelogram.

(a)

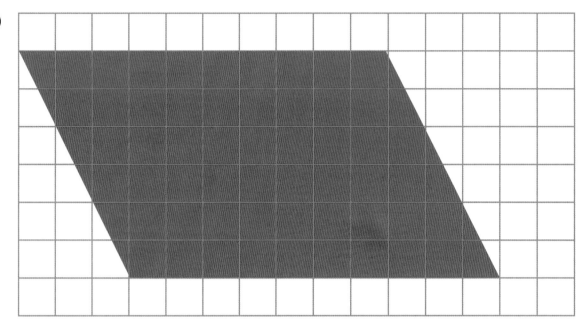

(b)

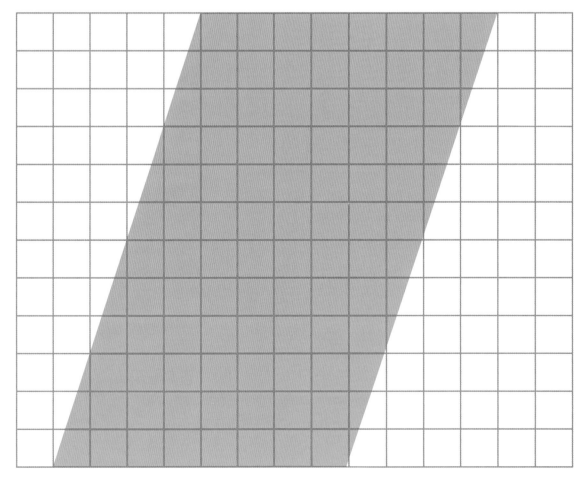

(c)

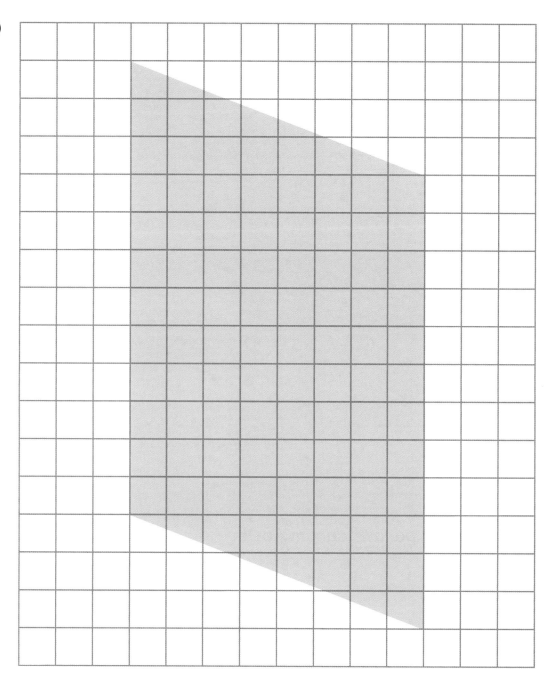

2

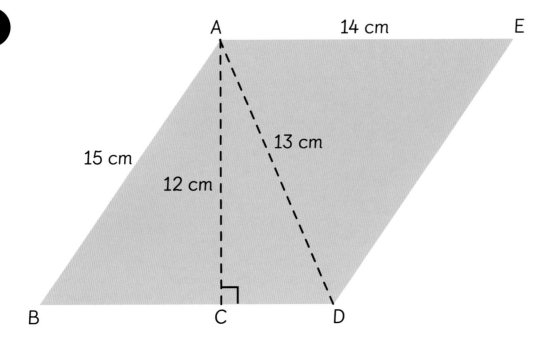

AB = 15 cm

AC = 12 cm

AD = 13 cm

AE = 14 cm

Find the area of parallelogram ABDE.

Complete Worksheet **6** – Page **77 – 78**

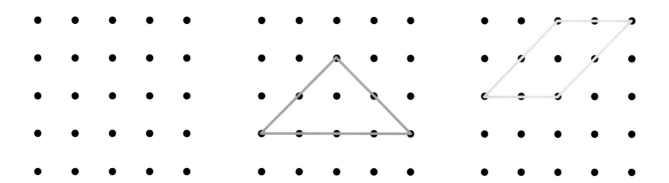

Draw some triangles and quadrilaterals on square dotty paper. The vertices must be at dots, and each shape should have only one dot inside.

Figure number	Number of dots on edges and vertices, n	Area in units², A
1	8	
2		

1 Count the number of dots on the edges and vertices of each figure.
Let this be n.

2 Find the area of the figure.
Let this be A.

Investigate how A and n are related.

Maths Journal

Two figures with the same area can have different perimeters.

A rectangle and another polygon that is not a rectangle can have the same area and the same perimeter.

Two figures with the same perimeter can have different areas.

Explain if each of them is correct by giving examples.

I know how to...

☐ find the perimeter and the area of rectangles, triangles and parallelograms.

☐ use formulae to find the area of rectangles, triangles and parallelograms.

☐ use the area of rectangles to find the area of other types of polygons.

Do you know how to find the volume of each solid?

Chapter 11
Volume

Finding the Volume of Cubes and Cuboids

In Focus

Make a cuboid or a cube using these small cubes.

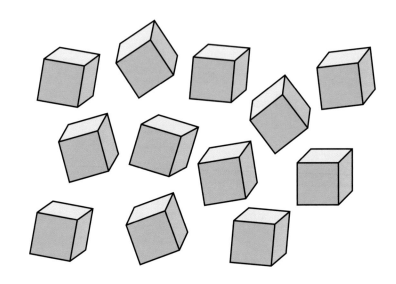

Let's Learn

1 makes this.

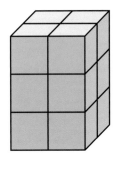

This cuboid takes up the same amount of space as 12 small cubes.

 takes up 1 cubic centimetre of space.

 's cuboid has a volume of 12 cm³.

 1 cm³

1 cubic centimetre

2 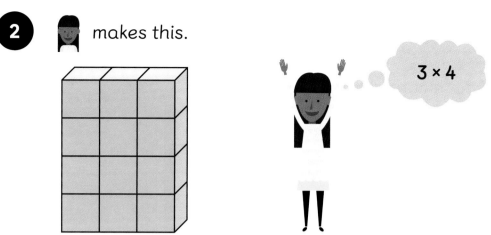 makes this.

Volume = 12 cm³

3 × 4

3 makes this.

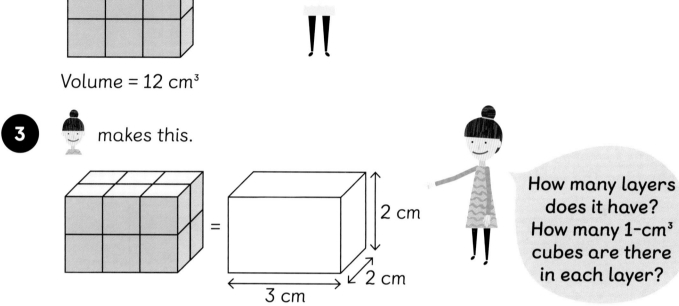

2 cm

2 cm

3 cm

How many layers does it have? How many 1-cm³ cubes are there in each layer?

Volume = 12 cm³

4 thinks he can make a cuboid that has the same volume as this.

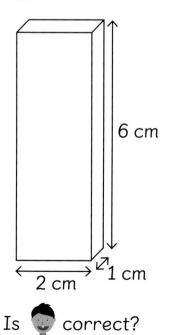

6 cm

2 cm

1 cm

Is correct?

What can you say about the volumes of the solids they made?

Guided Practice

1 Find the volume of each cuboid.

(a)

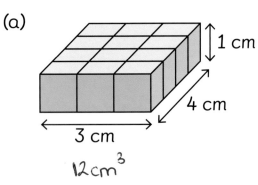

3 cm

4 cm

1 cm

12cm³

(b)

24 cm³

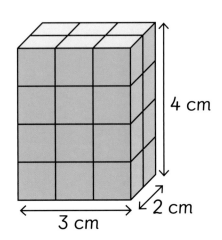

4 cm

3 cm

2 cm

2 Find the volume of each cube or cuboid.

(a)

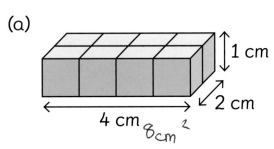

4 cm

2 cm

1 cm

8cm²

(b)

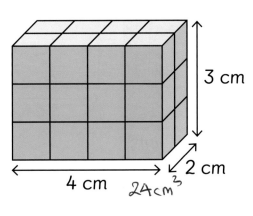

4 cm

3 cm

2 cm

24cm³

(c)

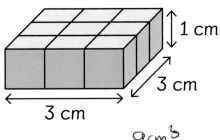

3 cm

3 cm

3 cm

27cm³

(d)

3 cm

3 cm

1 cm

9cm³

How is the volume of a solid related to its dimensions?

Complete Worksheet **1** – Page **89 – 90**

Finding the Volume of Cubes and Cuboids

In Focus

The red solid occupies much more space. It is so much taller.

Do you agree?

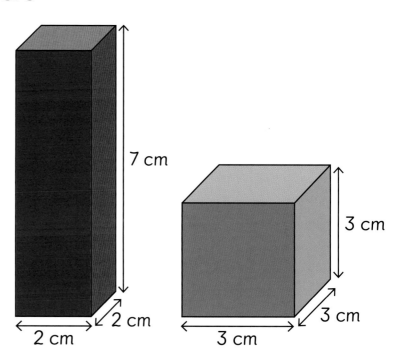

7 cm

2 cm

2 cm

3 cm

3 cm

3 cm

Let's Learn

1 Calculate the volume of the cuboid.

7 layers

2 × 2 1-cm³ cubes in each layer

volume = (2 × 2 × 7) cm³

= (4 × 7) cm³

= 28 cm³

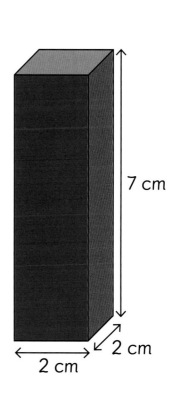

7 cm

2 cm

2 cm

2 Calculate the volume of the cuboid.

3 layers

3 × 3 1-cm³ cubes in each layer

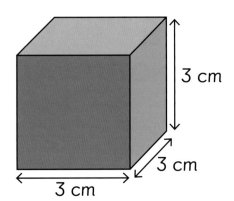

3 cm

3 cm

3 cm

volume = (3 × 3 × 3) cm³

= (9 × 3) cm³

= 27 cm³

The volume of the red cuboid is very slightly larger than the volume of the green cuboid.

The red cuboid is taller, so has more layers than the green cuboid; but each red layer has fewer unit cubes than each green layer so the two volumes are almost equal.

3 Write a formula to calculate the volume of a cuboid.

Let V = volume of the cuboid.

How many layers are there?

h

b

l

How many 1-cm³ cubes are there in each layer?

Let's consider the case where l, b and h are whole numbers.

$V = l \times b \times h$

Guided Practice

1 Estimate the volume of a box that can hold:

(a) a 1-litre bottle

(b) 50 £1 coins

2 Calculate the volume of each cuboid.

(a)

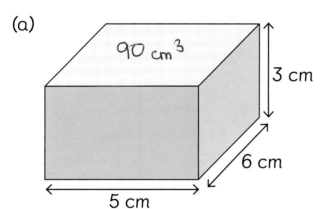

90 cm³

3 cm

6 cm

5 cm

(b)

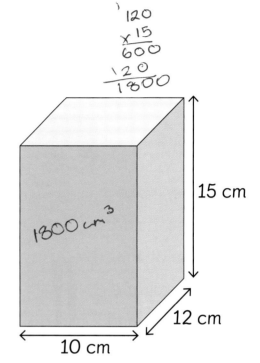

120
× 15
600
120
1800

15 cm

1800 cm³

12 cm

10 cm

3 Calculate the volume of each small cube.

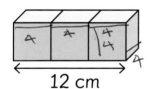

4   4   4
4
4

12 cm

12 ÷ 3 = 4

4 × 4 = 16
16 × 4 = 64 cm³

4 A vase is made by removing a cube from a rectangular block of clay.

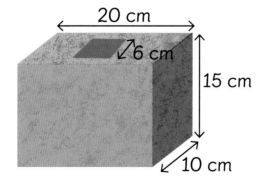

20 cm

6 cm

15 cm

10 cm

Calculate the volume of clay used to make the vase.

Complete Worksheet **2** – Page **91 – 92**

Finding the Volume of Cubes and Cuboids

In Focus

Using straws, make a cube whose inside has a volume of 1 m³. Estimate the volume of your classroom in cubic metres.

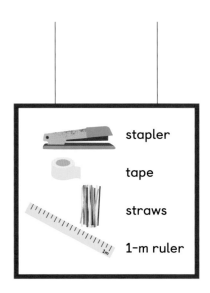

stapler

tape

straws

1-m ruler

Let's Learn

1 's idea

What is my idea?

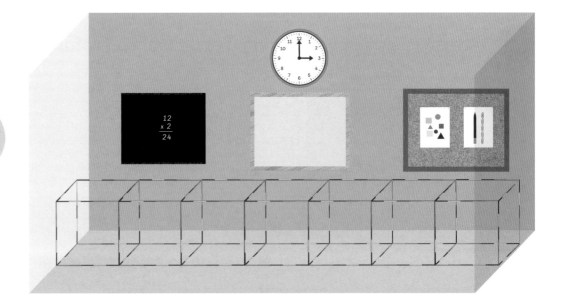

2 's idea

What is my idea?

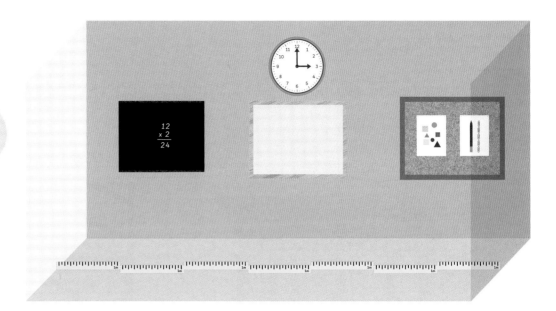

3 's idea

What is my idea?

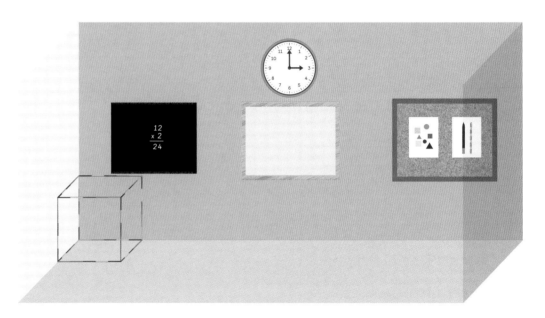

4 Estimate the volume of a classroom.

How many 1-m³ cubes fit in a row across the width of the room?

How many rows of these cubes fit in the floor space of the room?

How many layers are there to the ceiling?

What is the volume of your classroom?

Ours has a volume of about 210 m³.

Guided Practice

1 Estimate the volume of a box that can hold the following objects from your classroom.

(a)

(b)

2 Calculate the volume of each box.

(a)
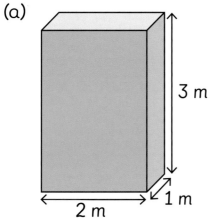

3 m

2 m

1 m

(b)
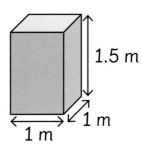

1.5 m

1 m

1 m

(c)
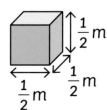

$\frac{1}{2}$ m

$\frac{1}{2}$ m

$\frac{1}{2}$ m

How big is each of these boxes?

Complete Worksheet **3** – Page **93 – 94**

Finding the Volume of Cubes and Cuboids

In Focus

 stacks several cubic boxes according to a rule. This is a 3-box arrangement.

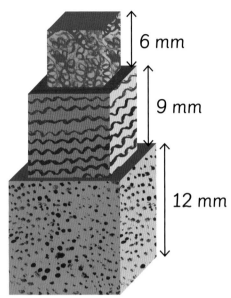

6 mm

9 mm

12 mm

Let's Learn

1 Calculate the volume of the smallest box in  .

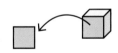

Measure the length of one side of the cube.

Six layers of 1-mm³ cubes can fit into the box.

volume = (6 × 6 × 6) mm³
     = (36 × 6) mm³
     = 216 mm³

$$\begin{array}{r} \overset{3}{3}\,6 \\ \times 6 \\ \hline 2\,1\,6 \end{array}$$

Each layer has 6 × 6 cubes.

 This means the box is 216 times as large as a 1-mm³ cube .

2 Calculate the volume of the largest box in .

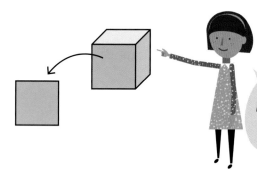

Measure the length of one side of the cube.

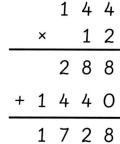

Twelve layers of 1-mm³ cubes can fit into this box.

Each layer has 12 × 12 cubes.

$$\text{volume} = (12 \times 12 \times 12) \text{ mm}^3$$
$$= (144 \times 12) \text{ mm}^3$$
$$= 1728 \text{ mm}^3$$

```
        1 4 4
    ×     1 2
    _____
        2 8 8
  + 1 4 4 0
    _____
    1 7 2 8
    _____
```

This means the box is 1728 times as large as a 1-mm³ cube .

I thought that a cube with sides twice as long would have a volume that is twice as large. I was wrong!

Guided Practice

1 Calculate the volume of this cubic box.

8 mm

How many layers of 1-mm³ cubes can fit in this box?

How many 1-mm³ cubes are there in each layer?

2 Calculate the volume of each rectangular box.

(a)

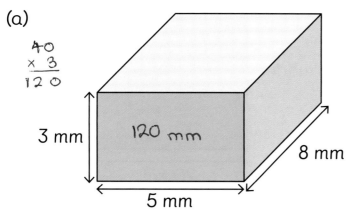

$\begin{array}{r} 40 \\ \times\ 3 \\ \hline 120 \end{array}$

3 mm

120 mm

8 mm

5 mm

How many 1-mm³ cubes fill each box?

(b)

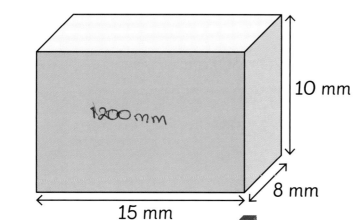

10 mm

1200 mm

8 mm

15 mm

$10 \times 8 = 80$

$\begin{array}{r} 80 \\ \times\ 15 \\ \hline 400 \\ 80 \\ \hline 1200 \end{array}$

3  adds two more cubes to , one smaller on top and one larger at the bottom to make a tower of five cubes following the same rule.

(a) Calculate the volume of the smallest box.

(b) Calculate the volume of the largest box.

Describe the rule that uses.

Complete Worksheet 4 – Page 95

Solving Problems Involving the Volume of Solids

In Focus

This solid metal cuboid is melted down to make cubes with 4-cm sides. Find the greatest number of cubes that can be made.

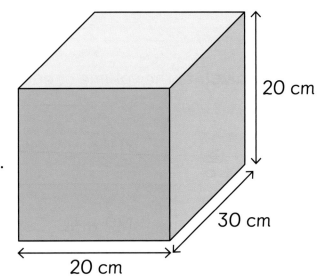

20 cm

30 cm

20 cm

Let's Learn

1 's method

$$\text{volume of metal cuboid} = (20 \times 20 \times 30) \text{ cm}^3$$
$$= 12\,000 \text{ cm}^3$$
$$\text{volume of each cube} = (4 \times 4 \times 4) \text{ cm}^3$$
$$= 64 \text{ cm}^3$$

$$12\,000 \div 64 = 187.5$$
$$\text{number of cubes} = 187$$

Why shouldn't I round it up to 188?

2 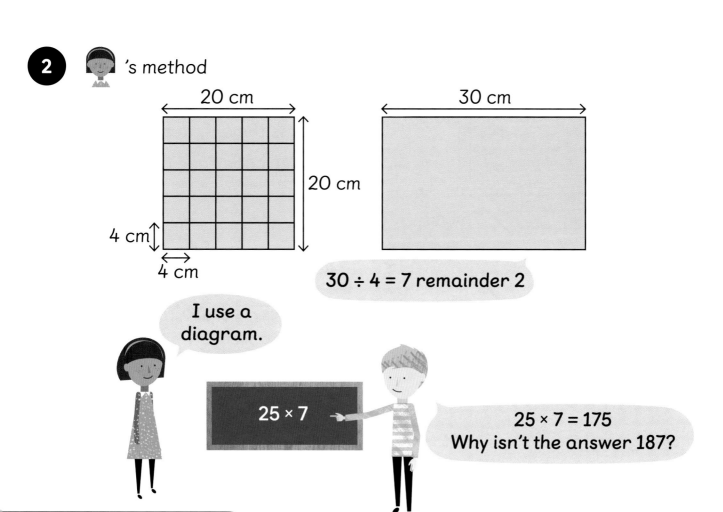 's method

20 cm

20 cm

4 cm

4 cm

30 cm

30 ÷ 4 = 7 remainder 2

I use a diagram.

25 × 7

25 × 7 = 175
Why isn't the answer 187?

Guided Practice

1 This tank is filled to the brim with water.

20 cm

30 cm

15 cm

How many 420cm³ bottles can be filled using the water in the tank?

2

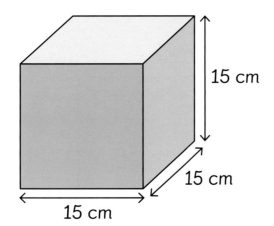

15 cm

15 cm

15 cm

A polystyrene cube is to be cut into smaller cubes with 4-cm sides. What is the greatest number of smaller cubes one can get?

3 A solid metal cube with 1-m sides is melted down to make smaller cuboids.

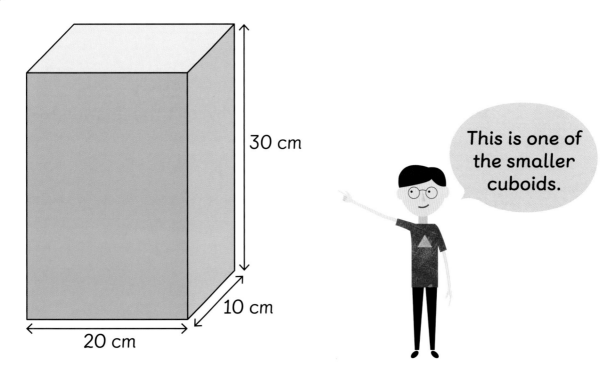

30 cm

20 cm

10 cm

This is one of the smaller cuboids.

Is it possible to make 167 cuboids like this one? Explain.

Complete Worksheet **5** – Page **96 – 97**

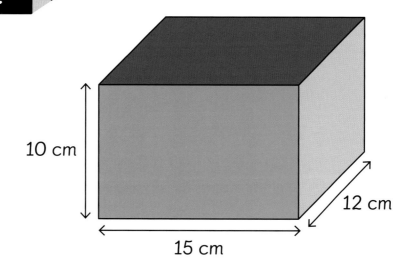

Find the greatest number of cubes that can fit into the box if each cube is:

(a) 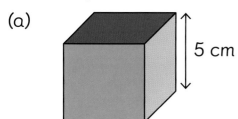 5 cm

(b) 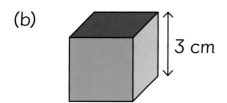 3 cm

(c) 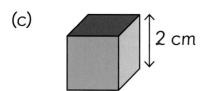 2 cm

(d) 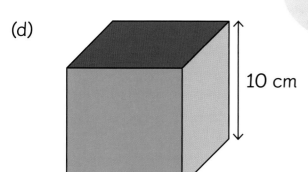 10 cm

Suppose 24 identical cuboids fill the large box exactly. Can you find the dimensions of each small cuboid?

What in the world has the following volume?

(a)   1 mm³

(b)   1 cm³

(c)   1 m³

(d)   1 km³

finds it difficult to imagine how large 1 km³ is. Write a note to explain how he can estimate the size of 1 km³.

I know how to...

Self Check

☐ find the volume of solids by counting unit cubes.

☐ calculate the volume of cubes and cuboids in standard units (mm³, cm³, m³ and km³).

☐ solve problems involving volume.

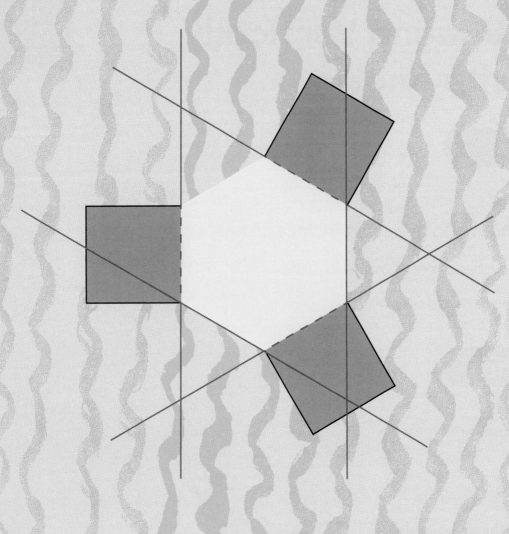

Can this be folded to make a box?

Chapter 12
Geometry

Investigating Vertically Opposite Angles

In Focus

 thinks that when two straight lines cross, the angles marked x and y are equal. How can we show this?

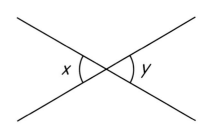

Let's Learn

1 did this.

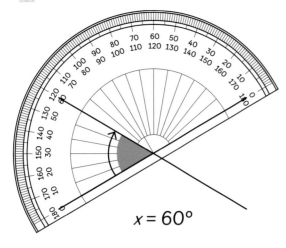

2 did this.

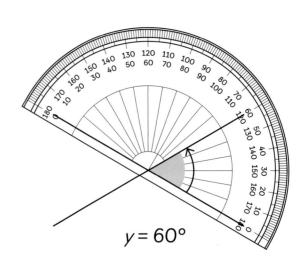

$x = 60°$

$y = 60°$

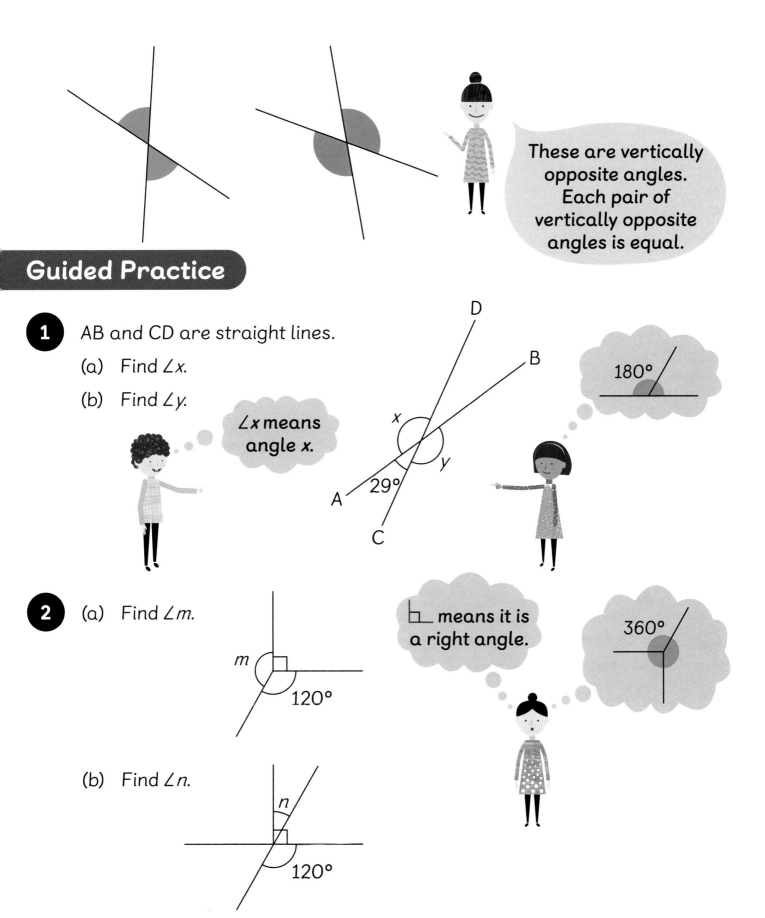

These are vertically opposite angles. Each pair of vertically opposite angles is equal.

Guided Practice

1 AB and CD are straight lines.

(a) Find ∠x.

(b) Find ∠y.

∠x means angle x.

180°

2 (a) Find ∠m.

120°

⌐ means it is a right angle.

360°

(b) Find ∠n.

120°

Complete Worksheet **1** – Page **101 - 102**

Solving Problems Involving Angles

In Focus

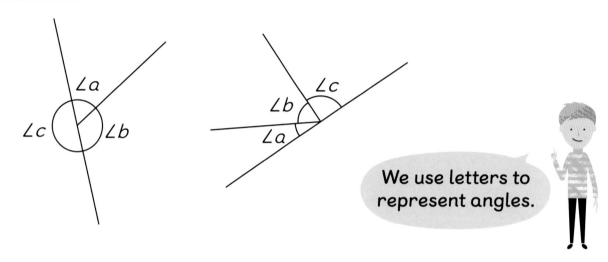

We use letters to represent angles.

The ratio of $a : b : c$ is $1 : 2 : 3$. What can we conclude?

Let's Learn

1 $a : b = 1 : 2$

This means angle b is twice as large as angle a.

2 $a : c = 1 : 3$

This means angle c is three times as large as angle a.

3 thinks it is possible to find the sizes of angles *a*, *b* and *c*.

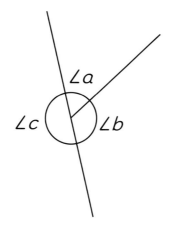

∠*a* means angle *a*.

∠*a* + ∠*b* + ∠*c* = 360°

angle *a*				
angle *b*				
angle *c*				

360°

6 units = 360°

1 unit = 360° ÷ 6

= 60°

∠*a* = 60°

∠*b* = 120°

∠*c* = 180°

thinks it is possible to find the sizes of angles *a*, *b* and *c*.

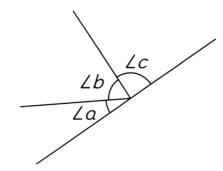

$\angle a + \angle b + \angle c = 180°$

angle *a*			

angle *a* ▭

angle *b* ▭▭

angle *c* ▭▭▭   } 180°

6 units = 180°

1 unit = 180° ÷ 6

= 30°

$\angle a = 30°$

$\angle b = 60°$

$\angle c = 90°$

Guided Practice

1 The ratio of the angle *x* to the angle *y* is 2 : 3.

(a) Find $\angle x$.

(b) Which other angle on the diagram has the same size as $\angle y$?

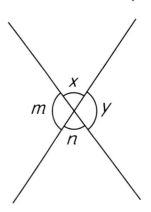

2 The angles *a*, *b*, *c* and *d* are such that:

- the sum of $\angle a$ and $\angle b$ is equal to a right angle
- $\angle c : \angle d = 4 : 5$

(a) If $\angle a = x$, write $\angle b$ in terms of *x*.

(b) If $\angle c = x$, write $\angle d$ in terms of *x*.

(c) Is it possible to calculate the values of $\angle a$, $\angle b$, $\angle c$ and $\angle d$?

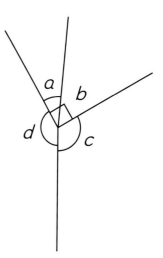

Complete Worksheet 2 – Page 103 – 104 ▶

Investigating Angles in Triangles

In Focus

The sum of the angles in a triangle is 180°. How can we show that?

Let's Learn

1 's method

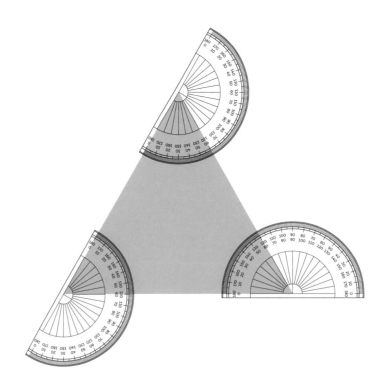

2 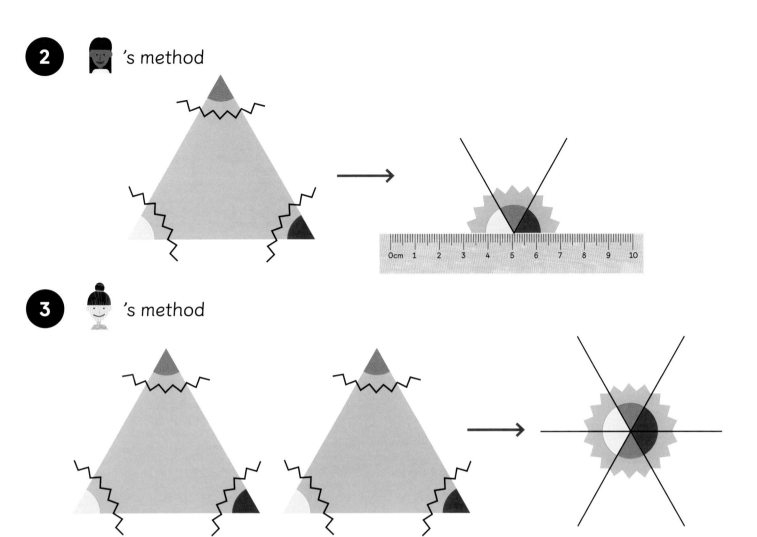 's method

3 's method

Guided Practice

1 ABC is an equilateral triangle.

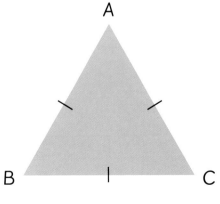

Find ∠ABC.

We name vertices using letters like A, B, C.

We name lines using a pair of letters like AB.

∠ABC means the angle between the lines AB and BC.

2 DEF is an isosceles triangle. Find ∠DEF.

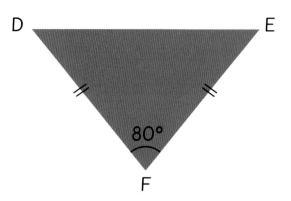

3 Find ∠GIH.

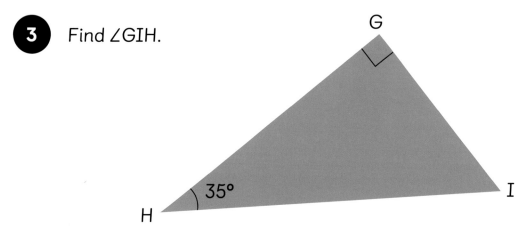

4 Find ∠JLK.

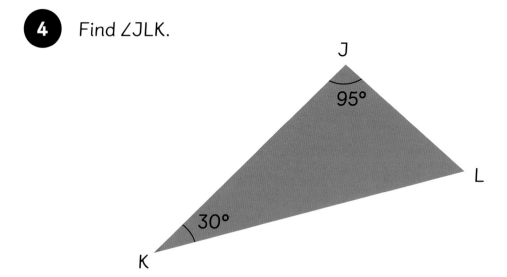

Complete Worksheet **3** – Page **105 – 106**

Investigating Angles in Quadrilaterals

In Focus

 Is correct?

The sum of angles in a quadrilateral is always 360°.

Let's Learn

1  's method

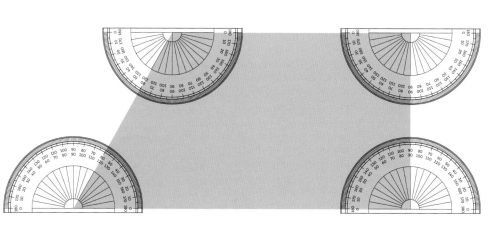

2 's method

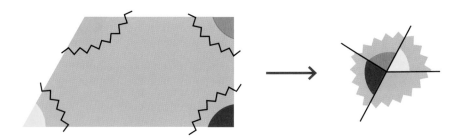

Guided Practice

1 (a)

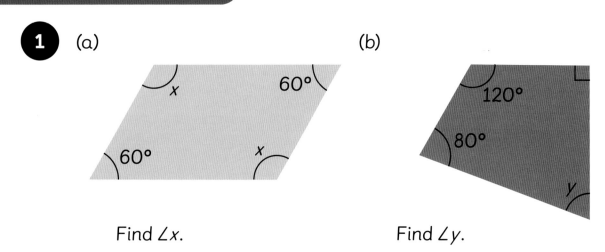

(a)

x $60°$

$60°$ x

Find $\angle x$.

(b)

$120°$

$80°$

y

Find $\angle y$.

2 Find $\angle AME$.

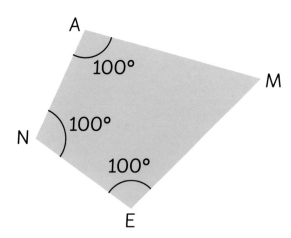

A

$100°$

M

$100°$

N

$100°$

E

Complete Worksheet **4** – Page **107 – 108**

Solving Problems Involving Angles in Triangles and Quadrilaterals

Lesson 5

In Focus

thinks that it is possible to find the values of *x* and *y*.

Let's Learn

1

180°

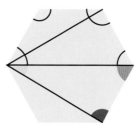

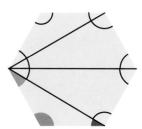

The 6 angles of the hexagon make up the angles of 4 triangles.

So the sum of these 6 angles is equal to 4 × 180°.

If all 6 angles are equal,

then   6*x* = 4 × 180°

    6*x* = 720°

    x =

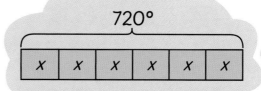

720°

x	*x*	*x*	*x*	*x*	*x*

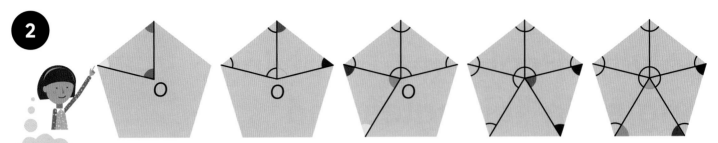

2

180°

The angles of the make up 5 triangles.

So the sum of the 5 angles of the pentagon + 360° = 5 × 180°.

If all 5 angles are equal,

then $5y = 5 × 180° - 360°$

              $5y = 540°$

                $y = $ ☐

Why do we subtract?

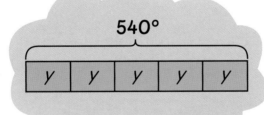

540°

| y | y | y | y | y |

1

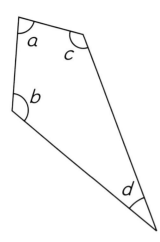

Find $\angle a + \angle b + \angle c + \angle d$.

2

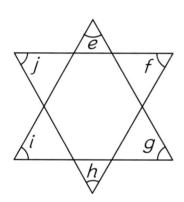

Find $\angle e + \angle f + \angle g + \angle h + \angle i + \angle j$.

3 Find the sum of the eight angles.

The figure consists of a square and 4 triangles.

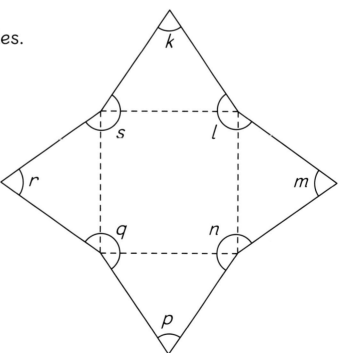

Complete Worksheet **5** – Page **109 – 110**

Naming Parts of a Circle

In Focus

This is a circle.

A circle is not a polygon.

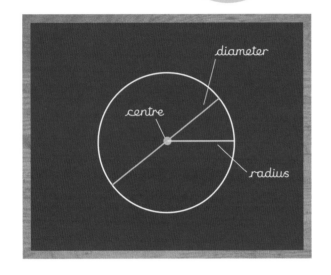

What can you say about the diameter of a circle with radius r?

Let's Learn

 1 looks at how the length of the radius and the diameter are related.

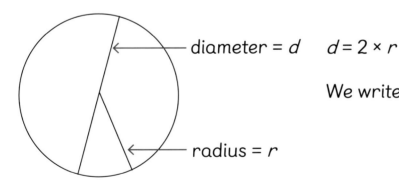

diameter = d $d = 2 \times r$

We write $d = 2r$.

radius = r

2r means 2 times r.

2 looks at how the length of the radius and the distance around the circle are related.

When $r = 1$ cm

For polygons, the distance round is called the perimeter.

For circles, it is called the circumference.

When $r = 2$ cm

When $r = 3$ cm

 uses and ⟞▭ to estimate the circumference of the circles.

Try it!

r	circumference, C
1 cm	
2 cm	
3 cm	

What do you notice about how r and C are related?

1 Find the length of the diameter, *d*, when the radius has length *r*:

(a)

$r = 4$ cm

(b)

$r = 2\dfrac{1}{2}$ cm

(c)

$r = 2.7$ cm

2 Find the length of the radius, r, when the diameter has length d.

(a)

$d = 6$ cm

(b)

$d = 5\dfrac{1}{4}$ cm

(c)

$d = 6.2$ cm

Complete Worksheet **6** – Page **111 – 112**

Solving Problems Involving Angles in a Circle

In Focus

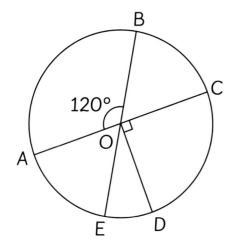

O is the centre of the circle.

AC = 14 cm

Which other angles can we find?

Let's Learn

1

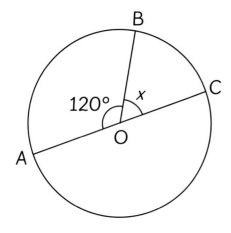

 finds ∠BOC.

$120° + x = 180°$

because AC is a straight line.

$120° + \boxed{} = 180°$

2

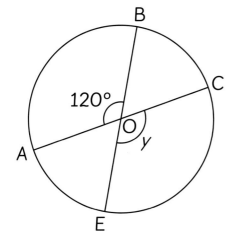

 finds ∠COE.

∠COE and ∠BOA are vertically opposite angles
so $y = 120°$.

3

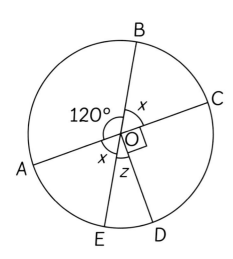

 finds ∠DOE.

Describe two ways to find ∠z.

1 (a)

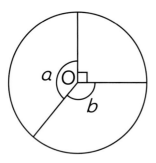

If ∠a = ∠b, find ∠a.

(b)

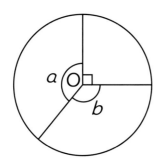

If ∠a : ∠b = 5 : 4, find ∠a.

2 O is the centre of each circle.

(a) Find ∠OBA, given that ∠AOB = 30°.

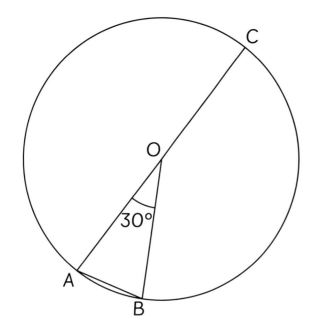

(b) Find ∠AOB, given that ∠OAB = 30°.

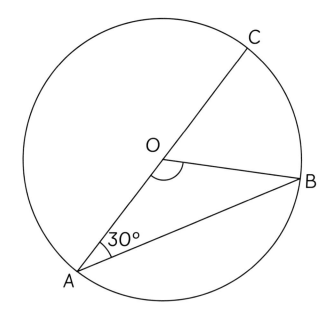

(c) Find ∠OAB, given that ∠COB = 30°.

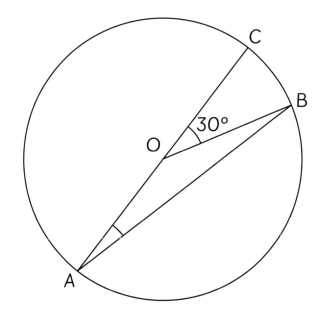

Complete Worksheet **7** – Page **113 – 114**

Drawing Quadrilaterals

In Focus

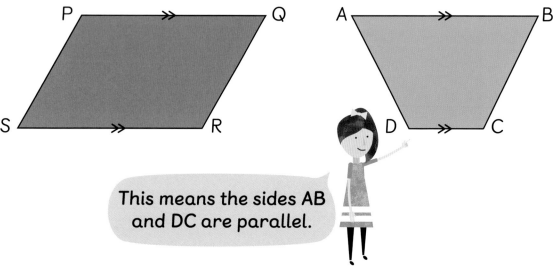

This means the sides AB
and DC are parallel.

draws two quadrilaterals.

Each has parallel sides that are 3 cm apart, PQ, SR and AB, DC.

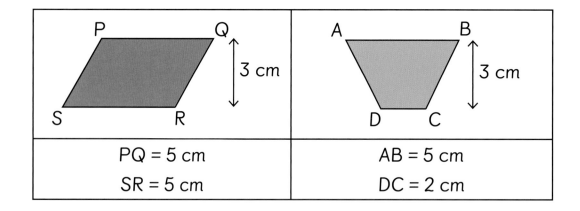

PQ = 5 cm SR = 5 cm	AB = 5 cm DC = 2 cm

Draw two quadrilaterals like this.

What do you notice about the other two sides of the quadrilaterals?

1 draws PQRS.

PQRS is a parallelogram.

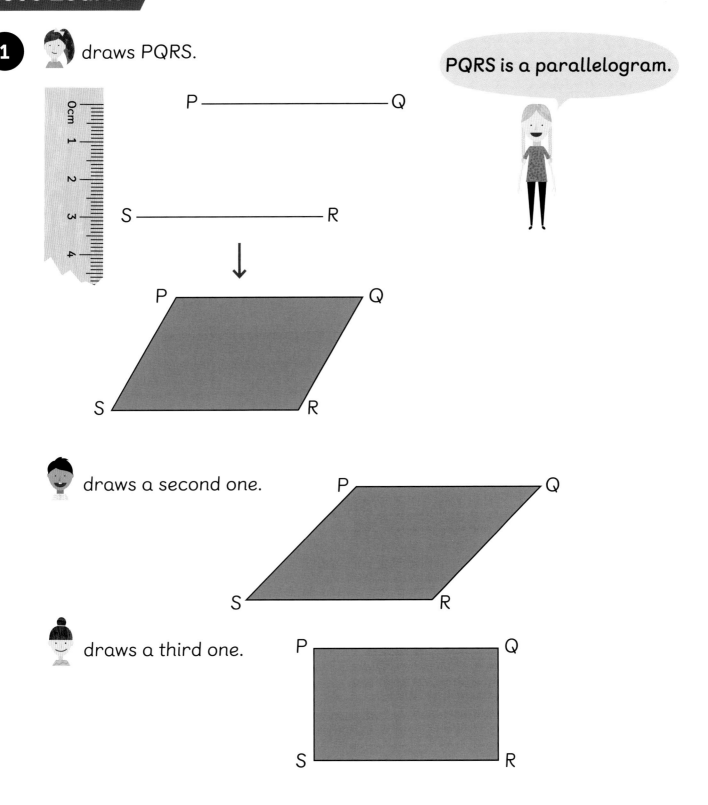

draws a second one.

draws a third one.

They have another pair of parallel sides that have the same length.

These are **parallelograms**.

2  draws ABCD.

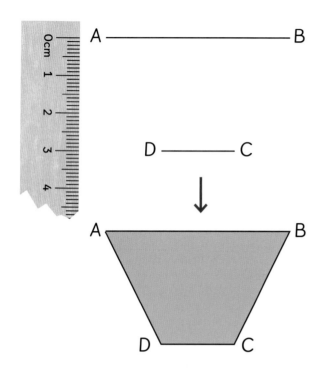

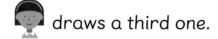 draws a second one.

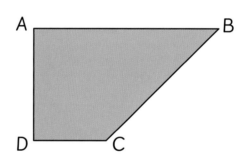

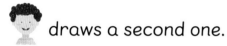 draws a third one.

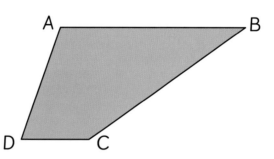

The other two sides are not parallel to each other.

These are **trapeziums**.

> Can the lengths of these other two sides be equal?

Guided Practice

1 Draw a right-angled triangle PQR with the measurements shown.

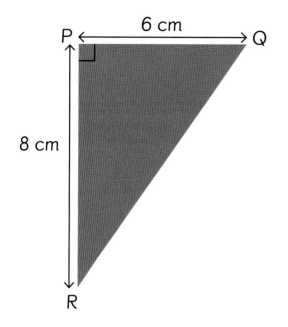

(a) Measure the length QR. Find the perimeter of the triangle.

(b) Measure the angles.

∠PQR	
∠PRQ	

2 Draw a quadrilateral STUV with the measurements shown.

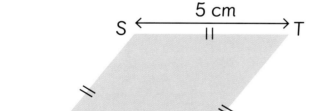

(a) Name this quadrilateral.

(b) Measure the angles.

∠VST	
∠STU	
∠TUV	
∠UVS	

Complete Worksheet **8** – Page **115 – 116**

Drawing Triangles

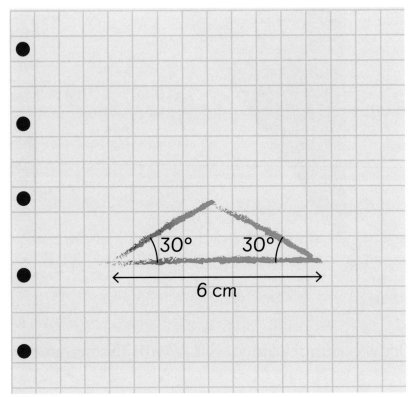

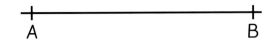 needs to draw this triangle.

Explain to how she can do it.

Let's Learn

Step 1: Draw a straight line 6 cm long using a ruler and pencil.

A   B

Step 2: Place a protractor to measure 30°. Mark X to show 30°.

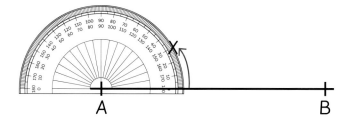

Step 3: Draw a line to show 30°.

Step 4: Do the same at B.

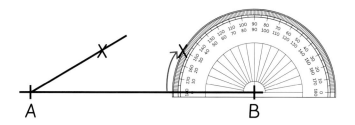

Step 5: Continue the two lines until they meet at C.

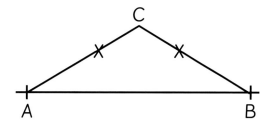

Draw each of the triangles with the measurements shown.

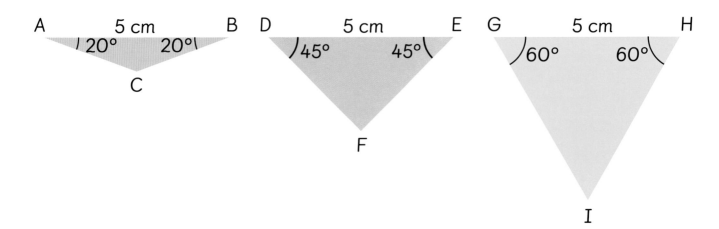

(a)   Measure the lengths of the two other sides.

(b)   Measure the third angle.

(c)   What do you notice about the triangles as the pair of angles increases?

Drawing Triangles

In Focus

   draw this triangle.

Their triangles look different.
Is this possible?

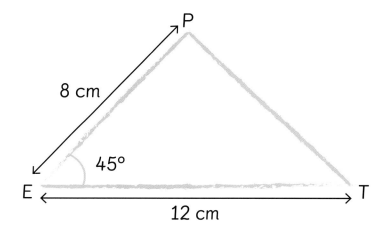

Let's Learn

1 uses a scale of 1 : 1.

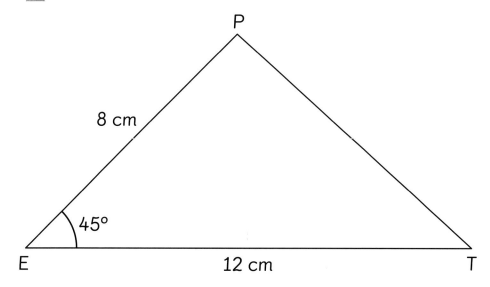

1 : 1 means 1 cm on the diagram represents 1 cm on the triangle.

2  uses a scale of 1 : 2.

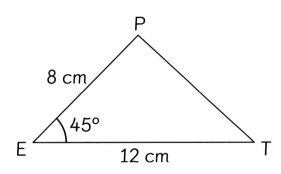

P

8 cm

45°

E   12 cm   T

1 : 2 means 1 cm on the diagram represents 2 cm on the triangle.

3 uses a scale of 1 : 4.

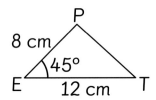

P

8 cm

45°

E   12 cm   T

1 : 4 means 1 cm on the diagram represents 4 cm on the triangle.

We say the three triangles are **similar**.

Guided Practice

1   (a)   Find the ratio of $a : b$.

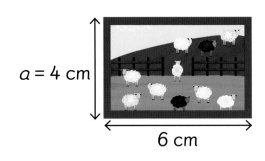

$a = 4$ cm

6 cm

$b = 8$ cm

12 cm

(b) Find the ratio of $x : y$.

$y = 3$ cm

$x = 15$ cm

2 The two triangles are similar.

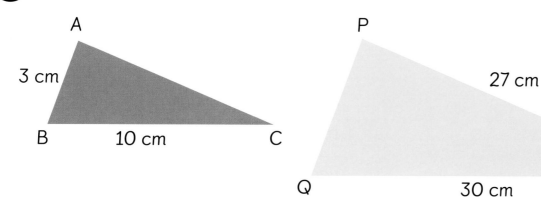

A

3 cm

B   10 cm   C

P

27 cm

Q   30 cm   R

The ratios of the lengths are:

AB : PQ = 1 : 3

AC : PR = 1 : 3

What is:

(a) the length of PQ?

(b) the length of AC?

Complete Worksheet **10** – Page **119 – 120**

Drawing Nets of Three-Dimensional Shapes

In Focus

This is a chocolate box.

It is a triangular prism.

Open up the box to get a flat shape.

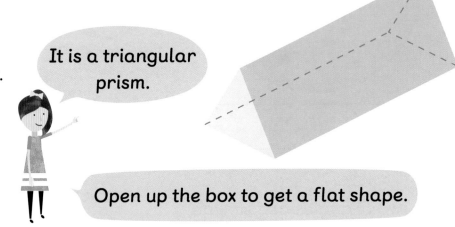

Draw a two-dimensional figure that can be folded to make this box.

Let's Learn

1

triangle faces

rectangle face(s)

2

This is a net of the box.

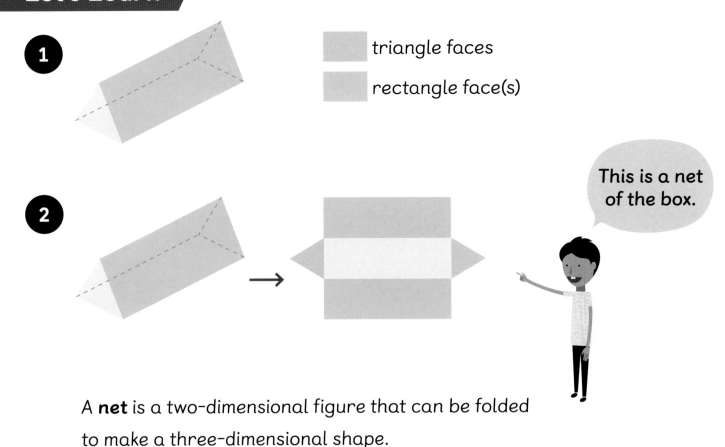

A **net** is a two-dimensional figure that can be folded to make a three-dimensional shape.

Work in pairs.

① Draw this figure.

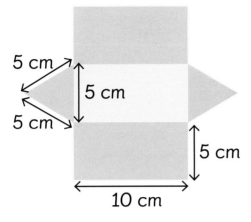

5 cm

5 cm

5 cm

5 cm

10 cm

What you need:

② Cut it out.

③ Fold it and tape the sides to make a box.

Guided Practice

1 This is a cylinder.

(a) Name the shape of the flat faces.

(b) When cut open and laid flat, the curved surface of the cylinder becomes a 2-D shape. What kind of shape is it?

2 This is a hexagonal prism.

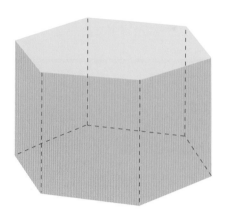

This is a net of the prism.

Use pattern blocks

to show other nets of .

Complete Worksheet **11** – Page **121 - 122**

Drawing Nets of Three-Dimensional Shapes

In Focus

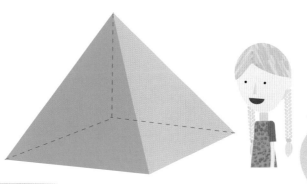

This is a square pyramid.

Open up the box to get a flat shape.

Draw a two-dimensional figure that can be folded to make this box.

Let's Learn

1

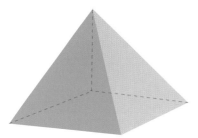

☐ triangle faces
☐ square face(s)

2

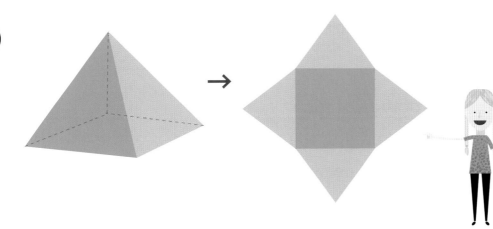

This is a net of the box.

Activity Time

Work in pairs.

① Draw this figure.

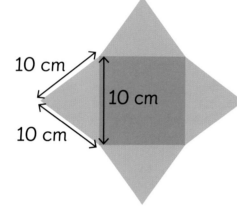

10 cm
10 cm
10 cm

What you need:

② Cut it out.

③ Fold it and tape the sides to make a box.

Guided Practice

1 This is a cone.

Look for an object around you that is a cone.

(a) Name the shape of the flat face.

(b) When cut open and laid flat, the curved surface of the cone becomes a 2-D shape with a part removed. What is the shape? What has been removed?

2 Match the solid with its net.

(a) (b) (c)

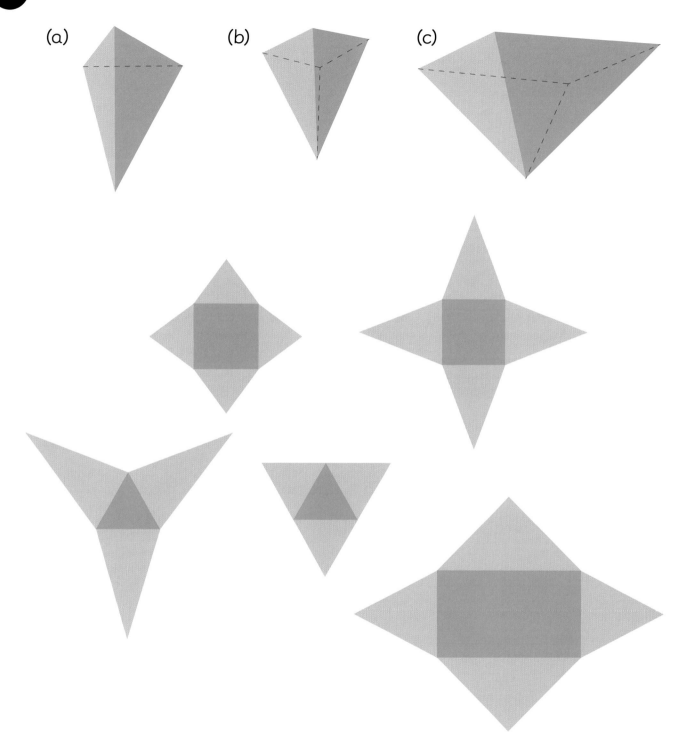

3 One net for each solid is shown.

(a)   (b)

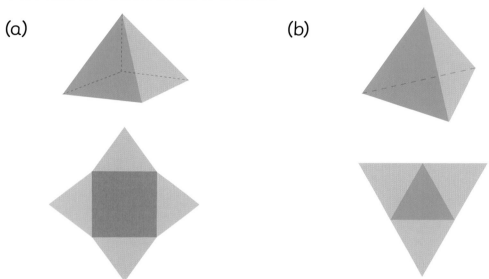

Use pattern blocks to show other possible nets for each solid.

Complete Worksheet 12 – Page 123 ▶

Mind Workout ▶

O is the centre of the circle. M, A and N are points on the circle.
Find the value of x.

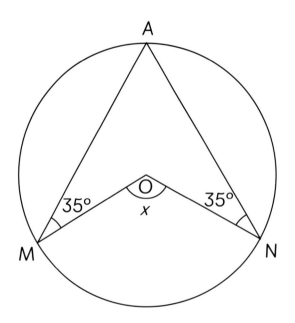

O marks the centre of each circle.

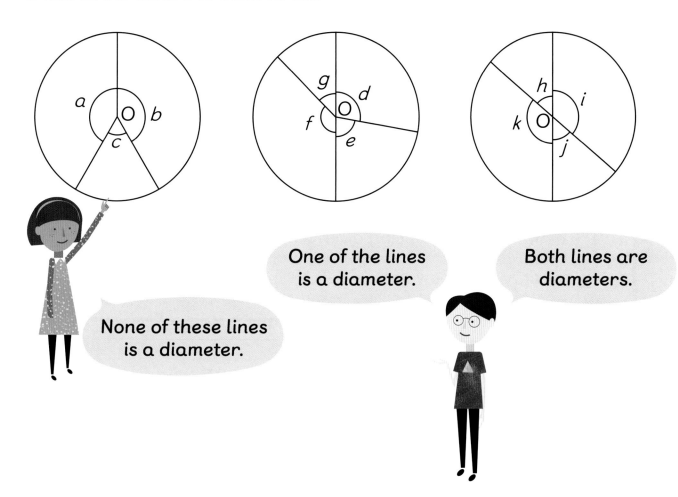

None of these lines is a diameter.

One of the lines is a diameter.

Both lines are diameters.

Write as many conclusions as you can about angles *a* to *k*.

I know how to...

☐ recognise angles that meet at a point, angles on a straight line, and vertically opposite angles.

☐ find unknown angles in triangles, quadrilaterals and regular polygons.

☐ identify the radius, diameter, circumference and centre of a circle.

☐ draw 2-D shapes using given dimensions and angles.

☐ identify and draw nets of 3-D shapes.

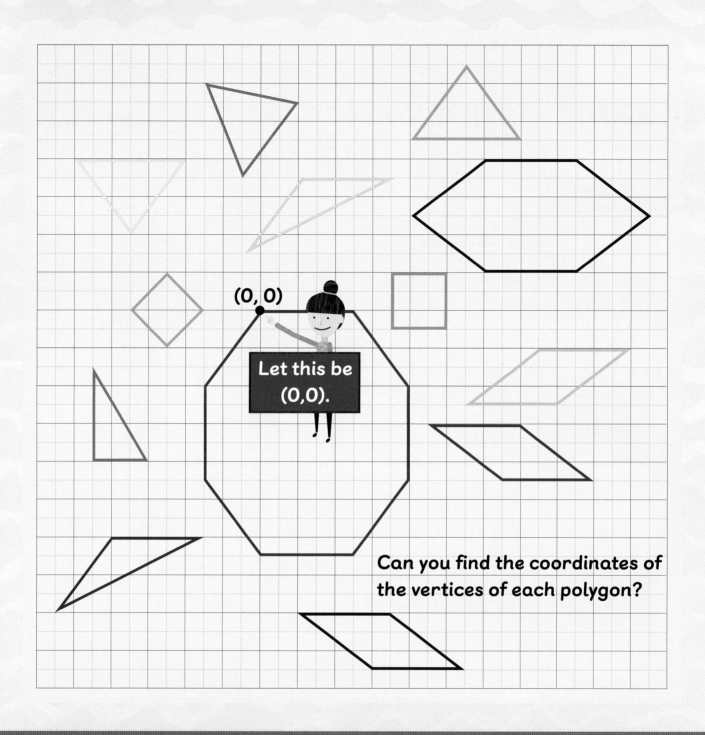

(0,0)

Let this be (0,0).

Can you find the coordinates of the vertices of each polygon?

Chapter 13
Position and Movement

Showing Negative Numbers

In Focus

The lowest and highest temperatures in Albany in the state of New York are shown.

What is the difference in temperature?

Let's Learn

1 Show −6 °C and 2 °C on a number line.

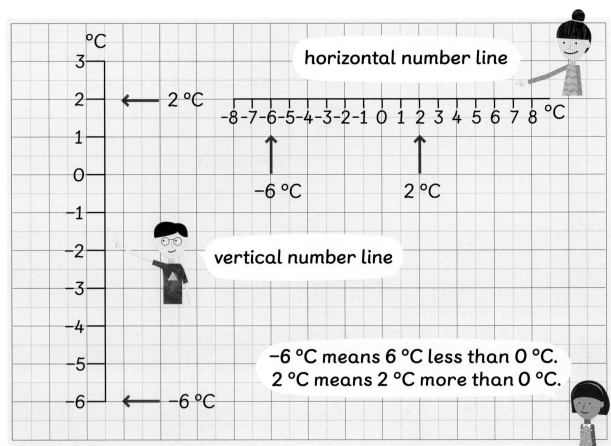

horizontal number line

-8 -7 -6 -5 -4 -3 -2 -1 0 1 2 3 4 5 6 7 8 °C

−6 °C   2 °C

vertical number line

−6 °C means 6 °C less than 0 °C.
2 °C means 2 °C more than 0 °C.

2 Find the difference between −6 °C and 2 °C.

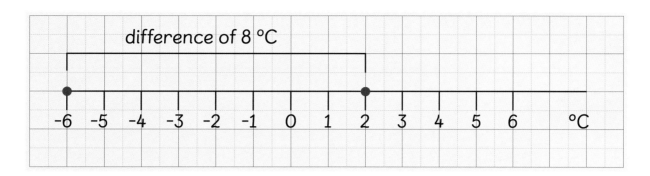

difference of 8 °C

Guided Practice

1 The diagram shows the water level in a lake.

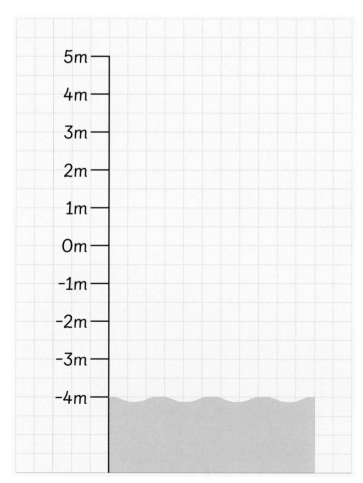

(a) What if the water level increases by 3 m? What is the final water level?

(b) What if the water level increases to 3 m? What is the increase in water level?

2

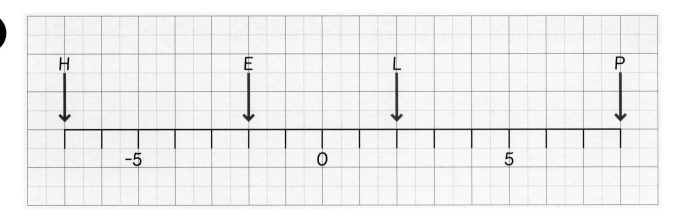

What number on the number line is shown:

(a) by point H?

(b) by point E?

(c) by point L?

(d) by point P?

3 Mark the point on this number line that shows:

(a) −3

(b) −1.5

(c) −0.5

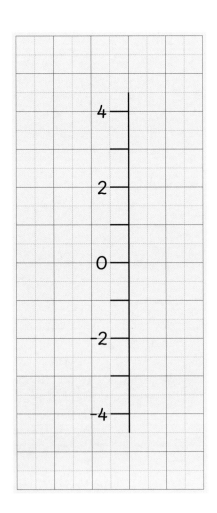

Complete Worksheet **1** – Page **129 – 130**

Describing Position

In Focus

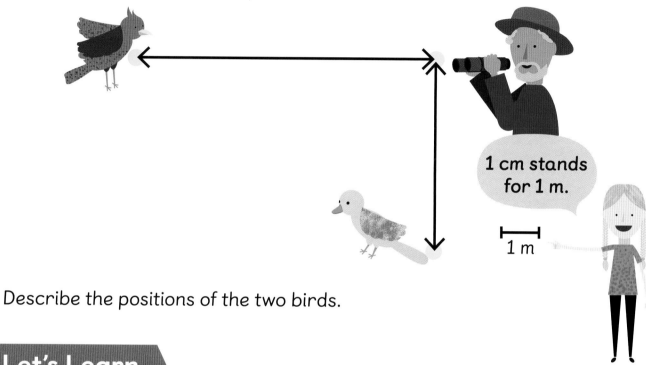

Describe the positions of the two birds.

Let's Learn

1

8 cm stands for 8 m

is 8 m from in a certain direction.

We can say is at $x = 0$ and is at $x = -8$.

2

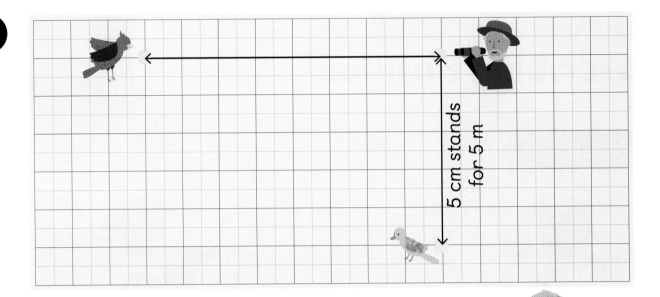

 is 5 m from in another direction.

We can say 🐦 is at $y = 0$ and 🐦 is at $y = -5$.

3

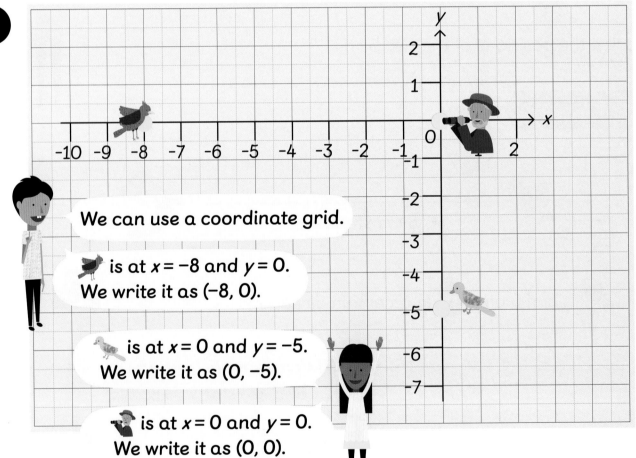

We can use a coordinate grid.

🐦 is at $x = -8$ and $y = 0$.
We write it as $(-8, 0)$.

🐦 is at $x = 0$ and $y = -5$.
We write it as $(0, -5)$.

🐦 is at $x = 0$ and $y = 0$.
We write it as $(0, 0)$.

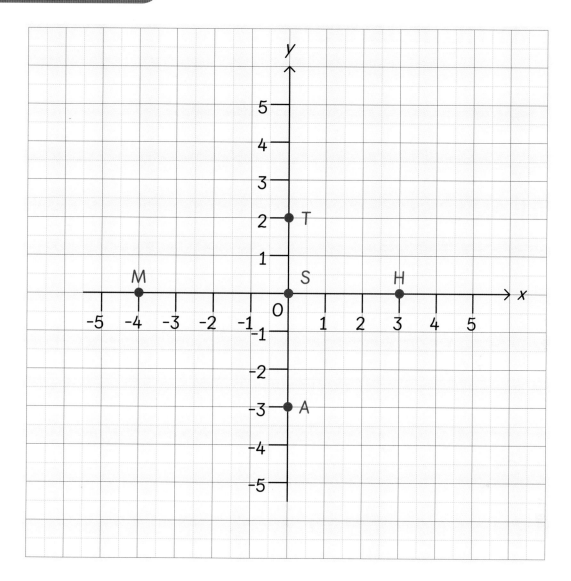

Write the coordinates:

(a) of point M

(b) of point A

(c) of point T

(d) of point H

(e) of point S

Complete Worksheet 2 – Page 131

Describing Position

In Focus

Can we describe the position of each point using coordinates?

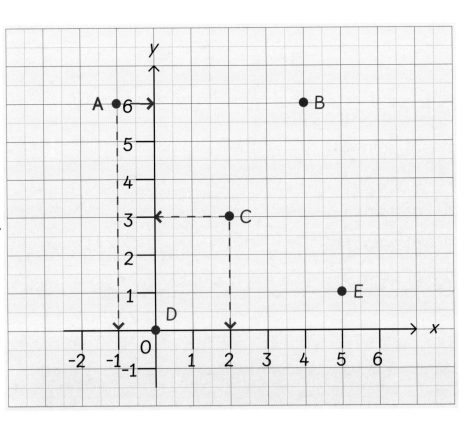

Let's Learn

1 lets D be (0, 0).

C is at $x = 2$ and $y = 3$.
C is at (2, 3).

A is at $x = -1$ and $y = 6$.
A is at (-1, 6).

B is at (4, ☐).

E is at (☐ , 1).

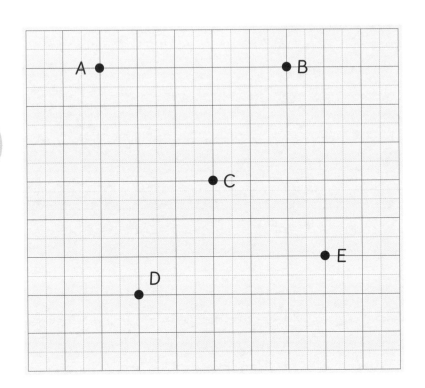

Position and Movement   Page 168

2 lets B be (0, 0).

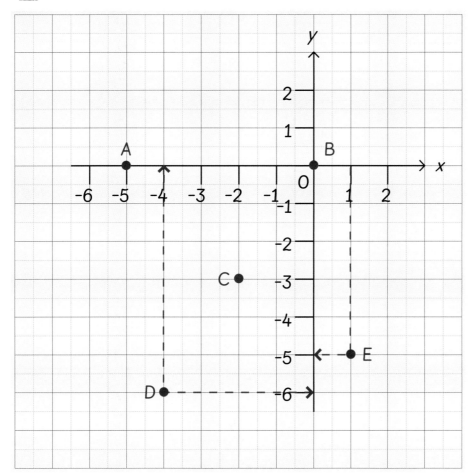

D is then at $x = -4$ and $y = -6$.

D is at (−4, −6).

E is at $x = 1$ and $y = -5$.

E is at (1, −5).

 A is at (−5, 0).  A is at (0, −5).

Who is correct?

C is at (,   ).

3 🧑 lets C be (0, 0).

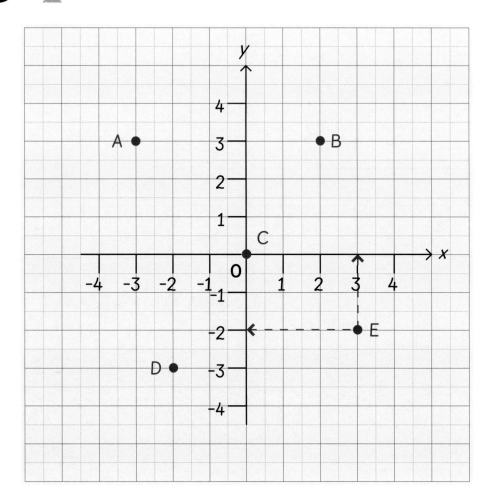

E is then at $x = 3$ and $y = -2$.
E is at (3, −2).

A is at (⬜ , 3).
B is at (⬜ , 3).
D is at (⬜ , ⬜).

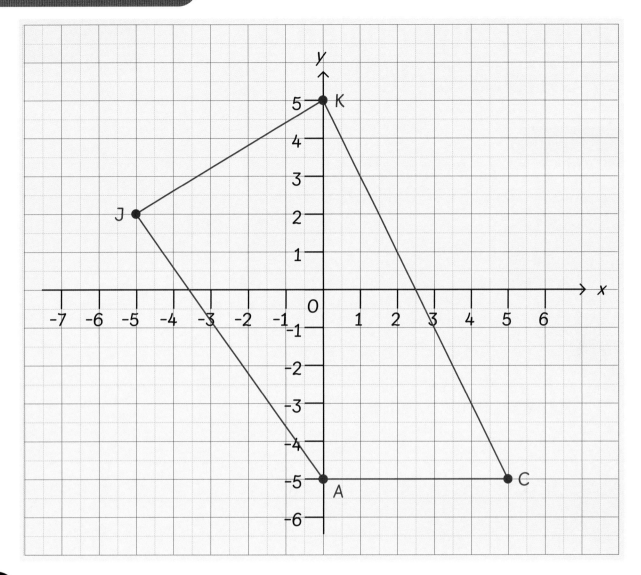

1 Write the coordinates:

(a) of point J

(b) of point A

(c) of point C

(d) of point K

2 Point M is such that Triangle MAC is an isosceles triangle. Write possible coordinates of Point M.

Complete Worksheet 3 – Page **132 – 134**

Drawing Polygons on a Coordinate Grid

In Focus

Part of a quadrilateral BEAR is drawn.

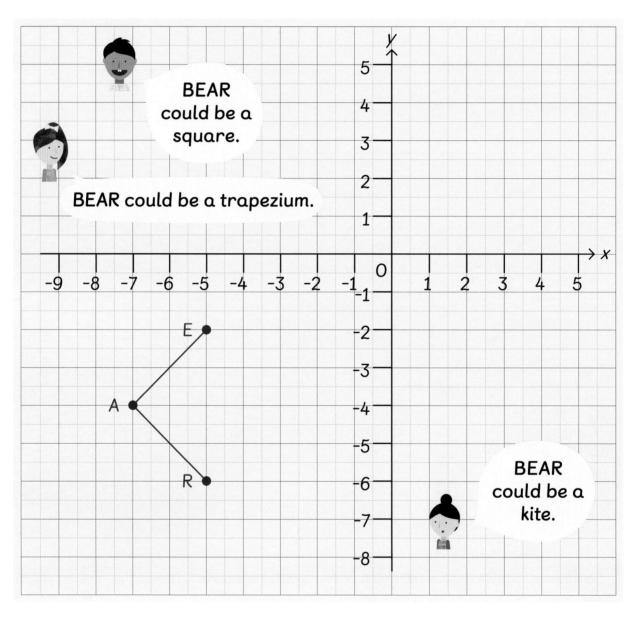

Who is correct?

1

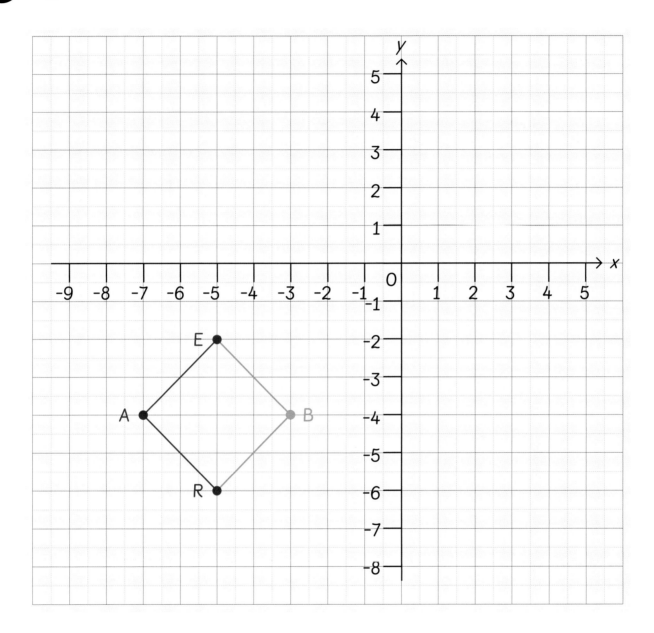

Quadrilateral BEAR is a square.

In this case, B is (−3, −4).

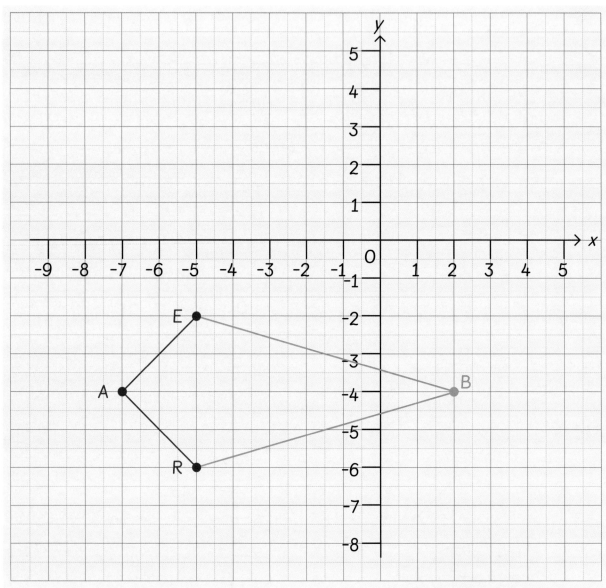

Quadrilateral BEAR is a kite.

In this case, B is (2, −4).

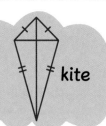

kite

Are there other possible positions for point B?

(0, −4)

(−2, −4)

(5, −4)

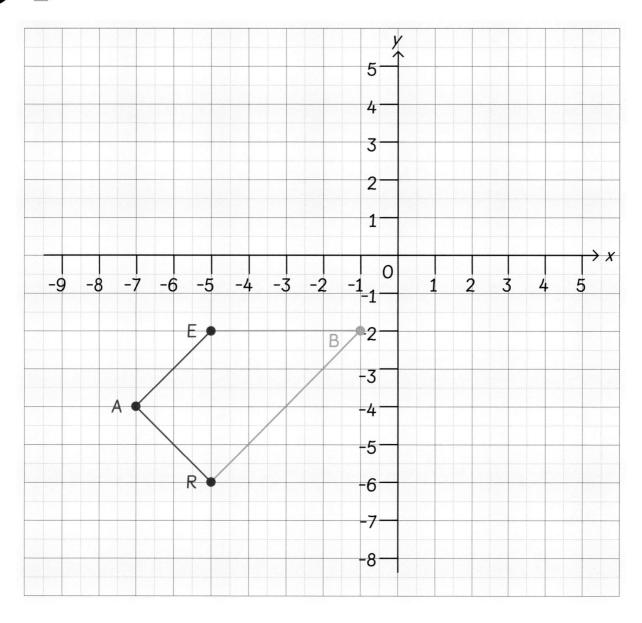

Quadrilateral BEAR is a trapezium.

In this case, B is (–1, –2).

Find other possible positions for point B.

(–4, –5)

(–4, –3)

(0, –7)

1

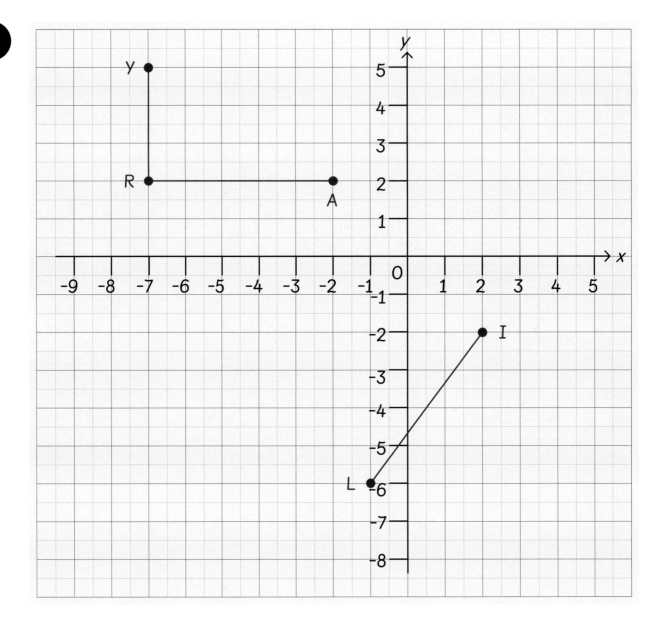

(a) Quadrilateral MARY is a rectangle. Write down the coordinates of point M.

(b) Quadrilateral LING is a rhombus. Find coordinates for point N and point G.

Is there more than one possible answer?

2 AN is one side of a polygon.

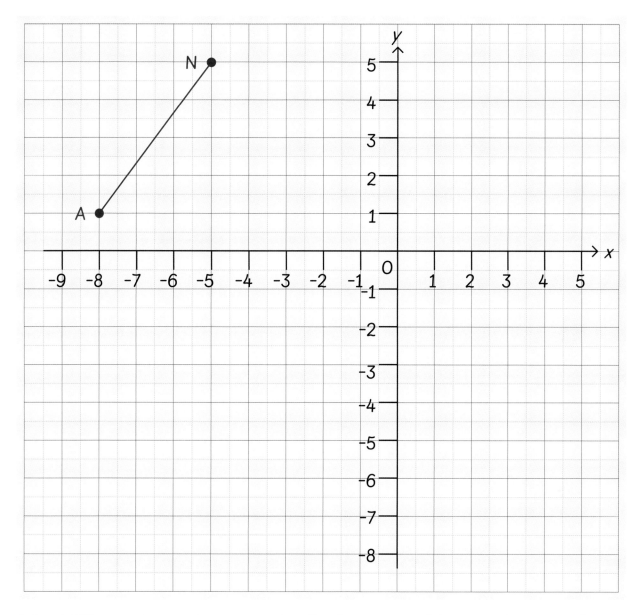

(a) ANT is an isosceles triangle. Find two possible coordinates of point T.

(b) ANT is a right-angled triangle. Is this possible?

Complete Worksheet 4 – Page **135 – 136**

Describing Translations

In Focus

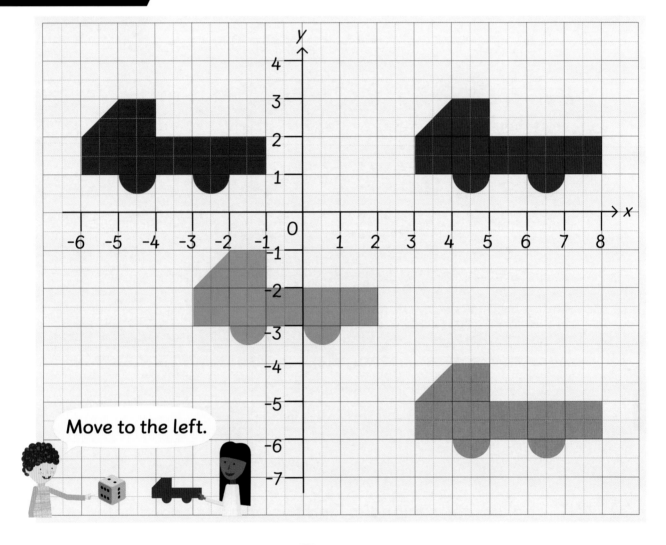

Move to the left.

1. Decide the starting position.

 blue

2. Decide the direction.

left

3. Roll a dice. Move the number of steps shown on the dice.

4. It is now your friend's turn.

5. The winner is the first player to move from one coloured figure to another.

1  starts from  .

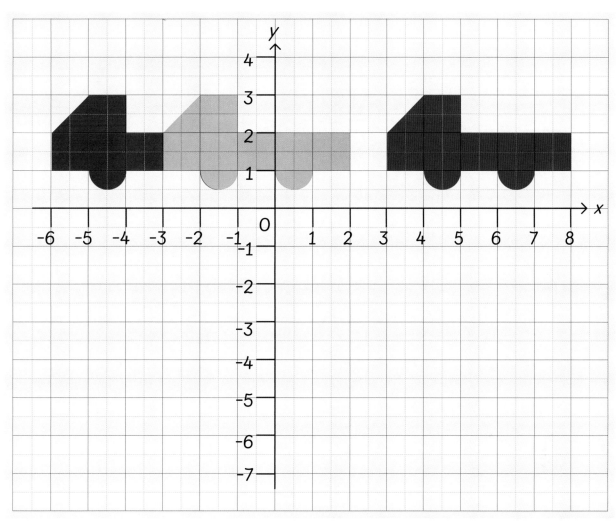

Move to the left.

Move to the left.

This type of movement is a **translation**.

What other combination of throws moves  to ?

2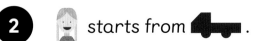

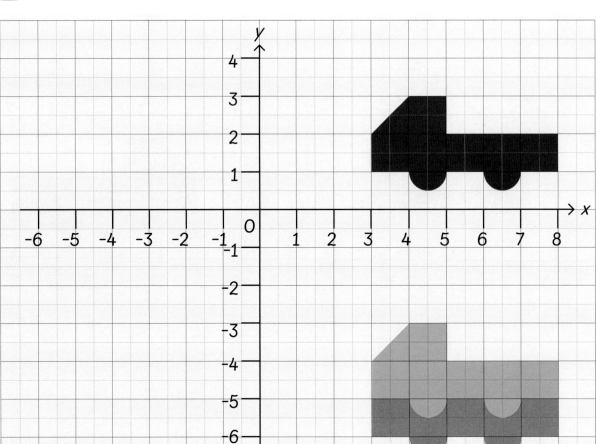

Move down.

How can  reach ?

3   starts from .

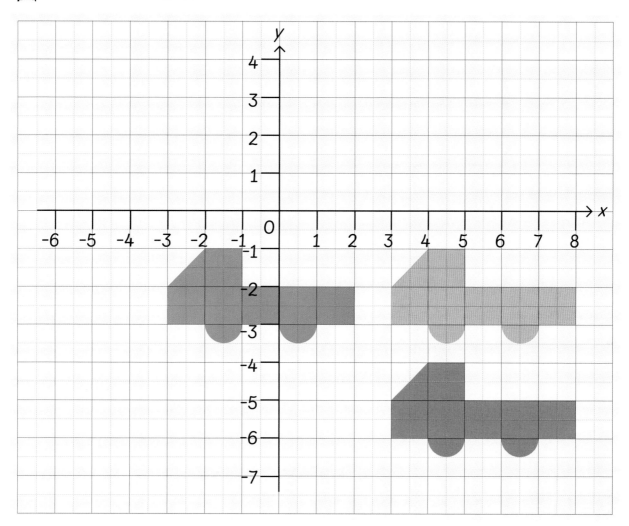

How can  reach ?

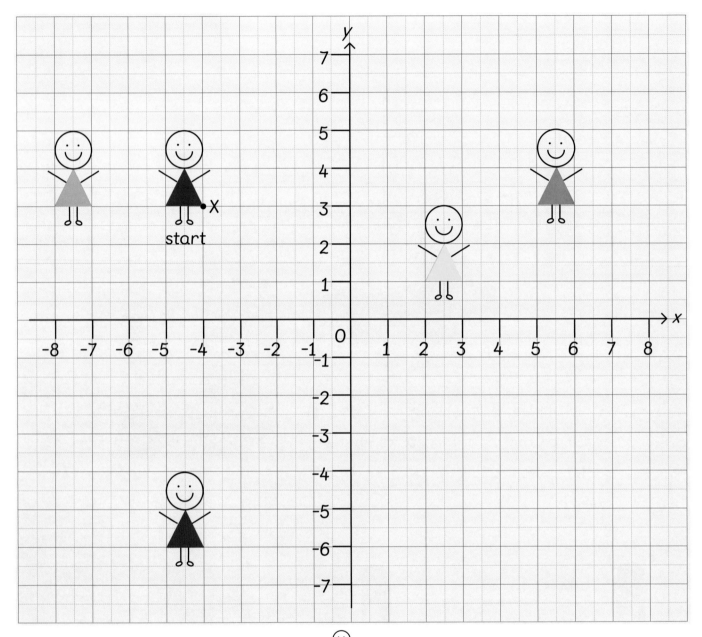

Describe the translation that moves :

(a) to   (b) to   (c) to   (d) to

In each case, state the coordinates of the position where X ends up.

Complete Worksheet **5** – Page **137 – 138**

Describing Reflections

In Focus

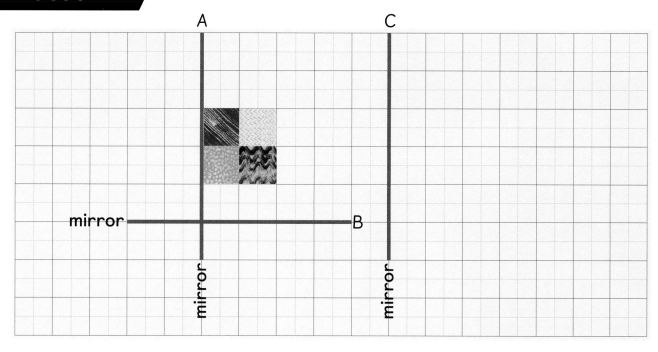

What do you see when you place a mirror on each line marked 'mirror'?

Let's Learn

 1

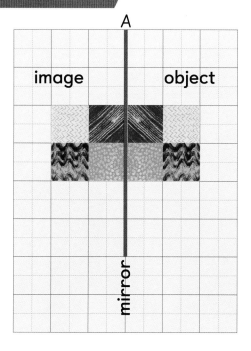

The image is the same size as the object in front of the mirror.

2

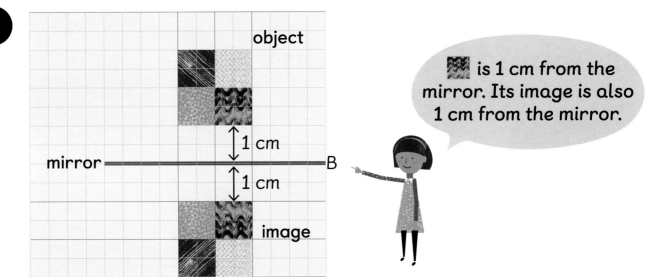

object

🌀 is 1 cm from the mirror. Its image is also 1 cm from the mirror.

mirror ─────────────── B

↕ 1 cm

↕ 1 cm

image

3

C

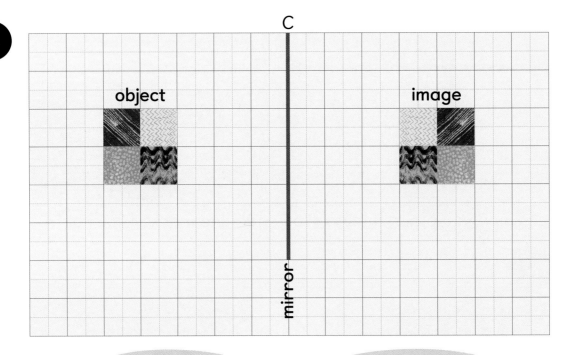

object

image

mirror

If the object is further from the mirror...

the image is as far away on the other side.

1 Draw the image of each letter.

(a)

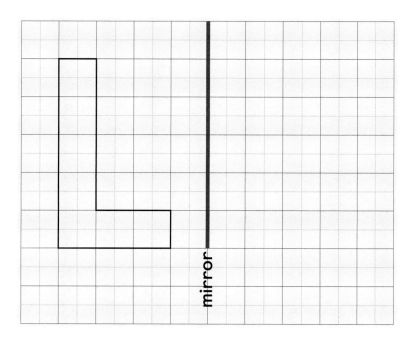

(b)

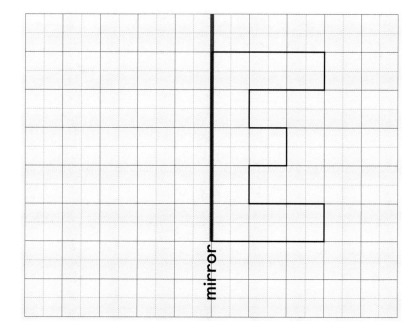

2 Draw the image of each letter.

(a)

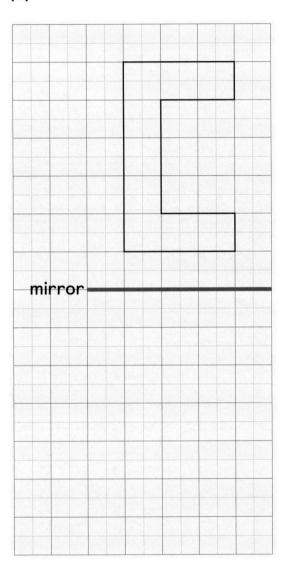

(b)

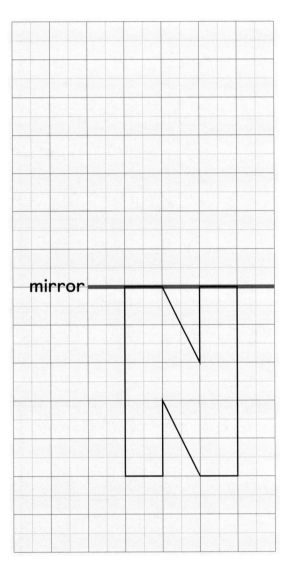

Complete Worksheet **6** – Page **139 - 140**

Describing Movements

In Focus

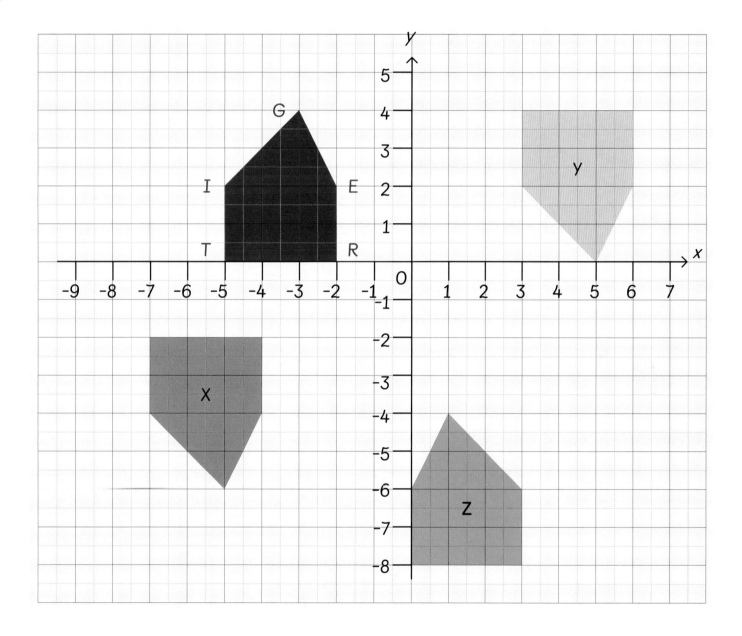

Is it possible to reflect the figure TIGER in the *x*-axis or in the *y*-axis so that the image is at X, or at Y, or at Z?

1 Reflect figure TIGER in the *x*-axis.

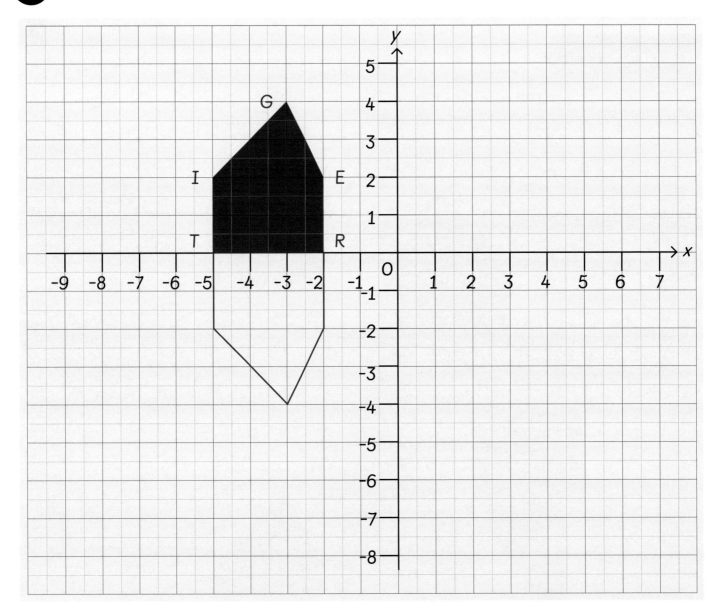

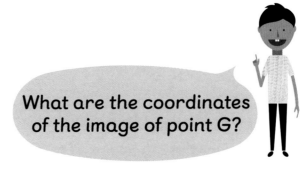

What are the coordinates of the image of point G?

Reflect figure TIGER in the *y*-axis.

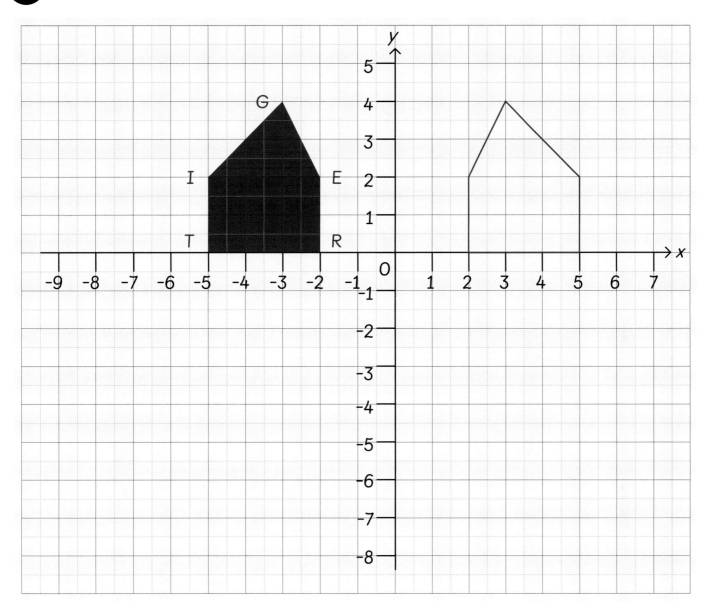

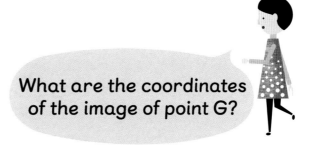

What are the coordinates
of the image of point G?

3 Where should figure TIGER start out so that the image is X?

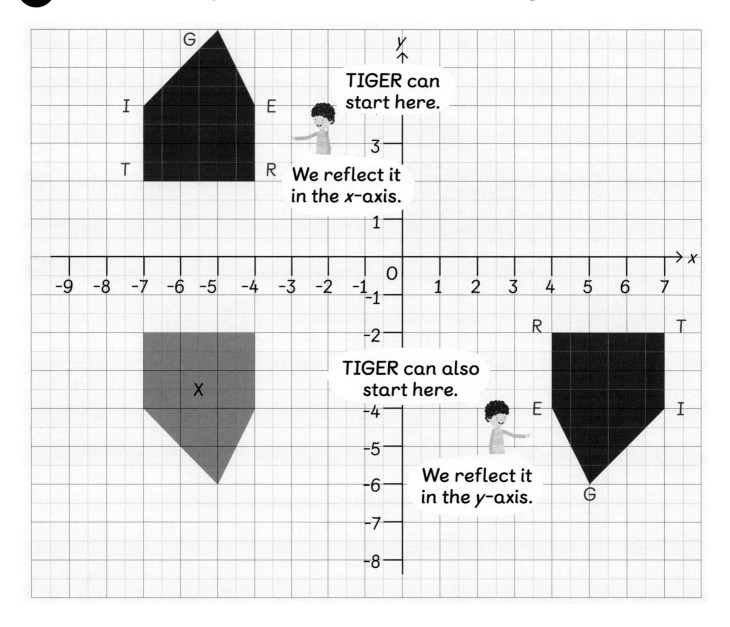

4 Where should figure TIGER start out so that the image is Y?

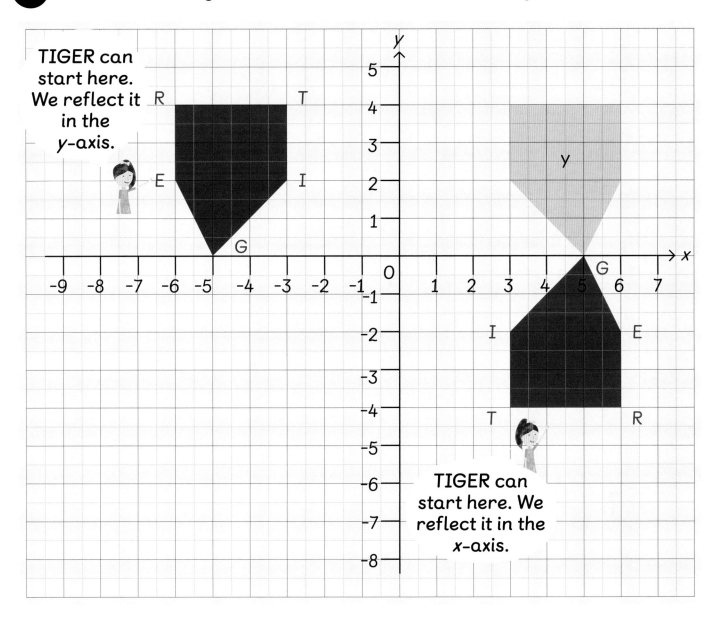

TIGER can start here. We reflect it in the y-axis.

TIGER can start here. We reflect it in the x-axis.

Where should figure TIGER start out so that the image is Z?

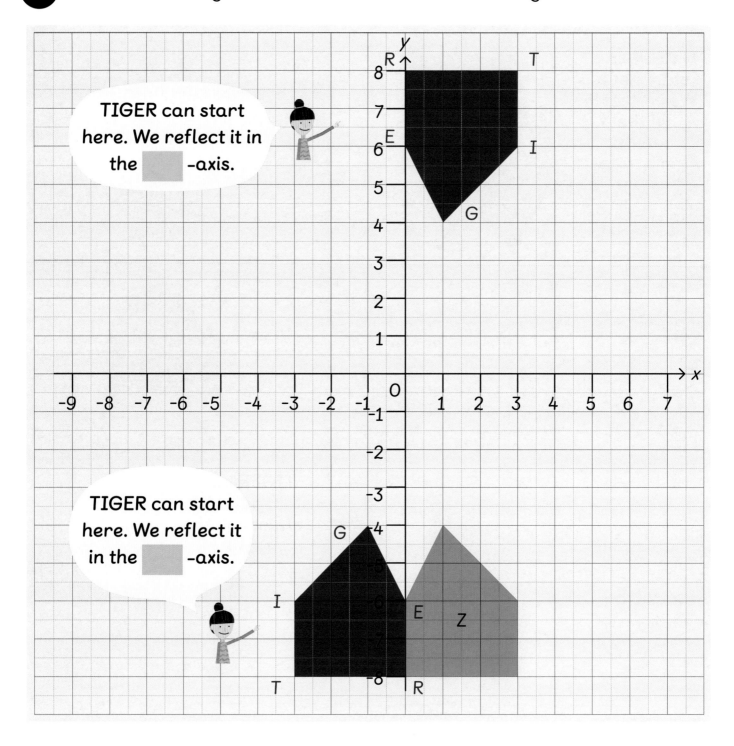

TIGER can start here. We reflect it in the ▯ -axis.

TIGER can start here. We reflect it in the ▯ -axis.

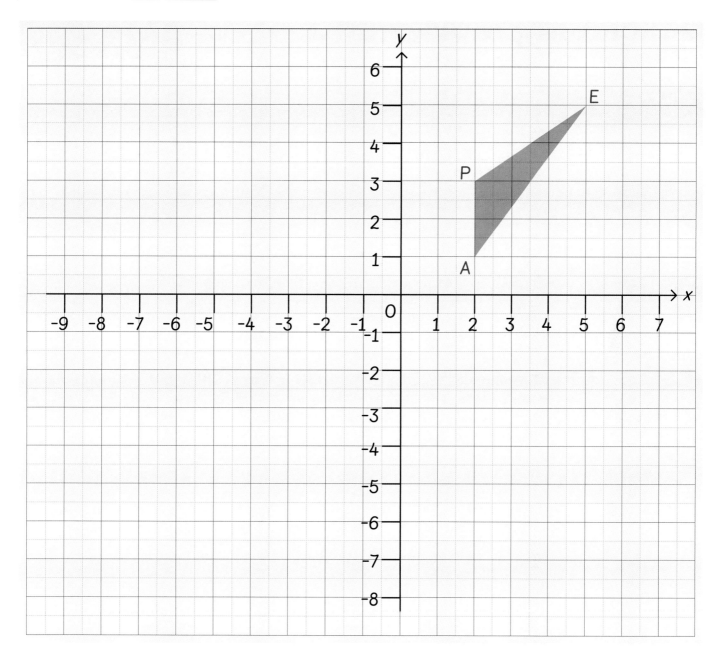

	reflect in x-axis	reflect in y-axis
A(2, 1)	(2,)	(,)
P(2, 3)	(, −3)	(,)
E(5, 5)	(,)	(,)

Complete Worksheet **7** – Page **141**

Describing Movements

In Focus

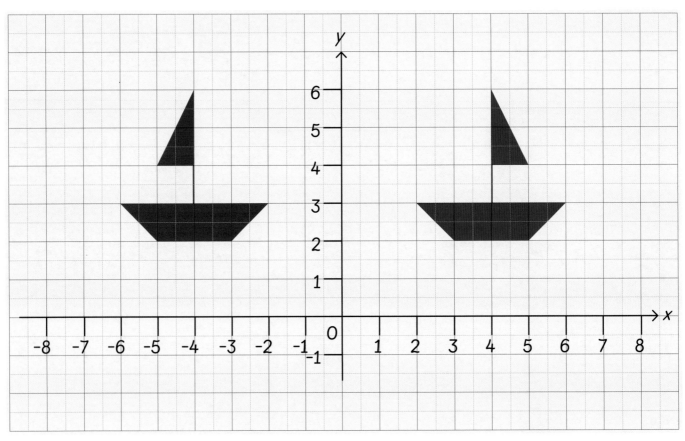

When the red figure is translated, it could end up where the blue figure is.

Is  correct?

Let's Learn

1 The figure is translated.

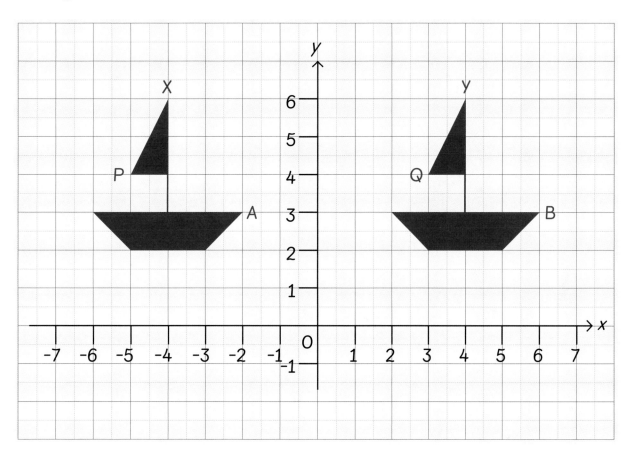

When the figure is translated to the right by 8 units,

A(–2, 3) ends up at B(6, 3).

P(–5, 4) ends up at Q(3, 4).

X(–4, 6) ends up at Y(4, 6).

> P(–5, 4) should
> end up at Q(5, 4).

> was not correct
> His figure was not translated.

2 The figure is reflected.

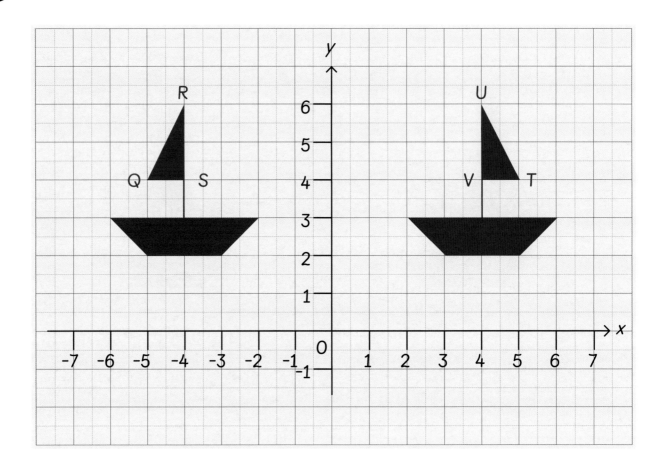

When the figure is reflected in the *y*-axis,

Q(−5 , 4) ends up at T(5, 4).

R(−4, 6) ends up at U(4, 6).

S(−4, 4) ends up at V(4, 4).

When the red figure is reflected, it ends up at the location where the blue figure is.

It is reflected in the *y*-axis.

1

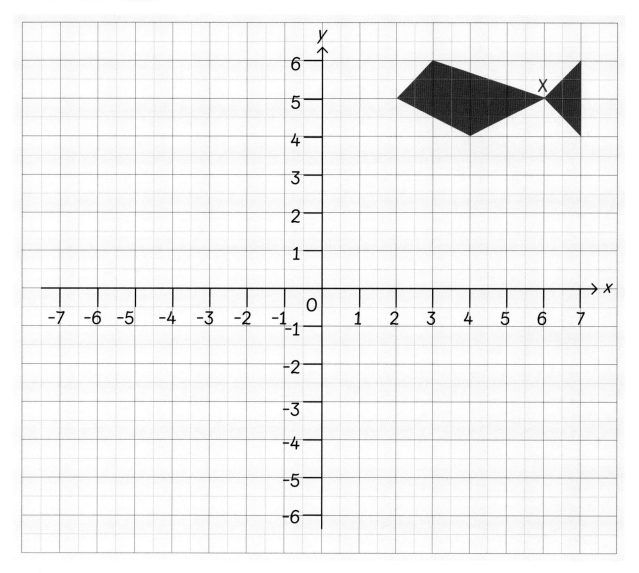

(a) Reflect the figure shown in the *x*-axis. Draw the image.

(b) Translate the figure shown 8 units downwards. Draw the image.

(c)   thinks that both (a) and (b) are the same movement.

Explain why is wrong.

(d) Another movement takes the point X(6, 5) to the point (−6, 5).

(i) Can the movement be a translation? Describe the translation.

(ii) Can the movement be a reflection? Describe the reflection.

In each case, find the coordinates of the vertices
of the quadrilateral after the movement.

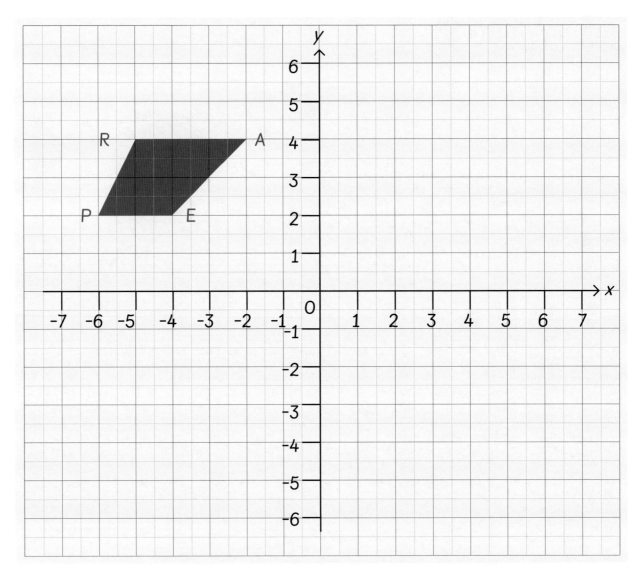

(a) Trapezium PEAR is reflected in the *x*-axis. Complete the table.

vertex	coordinates before reflection	coordinates after reflection
P	(–6, 2)	(–6, –2)
E	(,)	(,)
A	(,)	(,)
R	(,)	(,)

(b) Is it possible for P(–6, 2) to end up at (–6, –2) under a translation? If so, describe it.

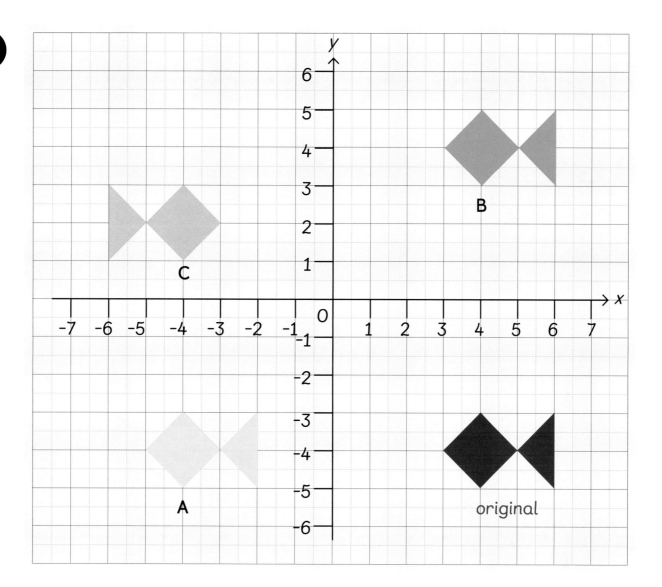

(a) Describe the translation that moves ◆◀ to the position shown by A.

(b) Describe the translation that moves ◆◀ to the position shown by B.

(c) Describe the reflection that moves ◆◀ to the position shown by B.

(d) Describe the translation and reflection that moves ◆◀ to the position shown by C.

Complete Worksheet **8** – Page **142 – 143**

Using Algebra to Describe Position

In Focus

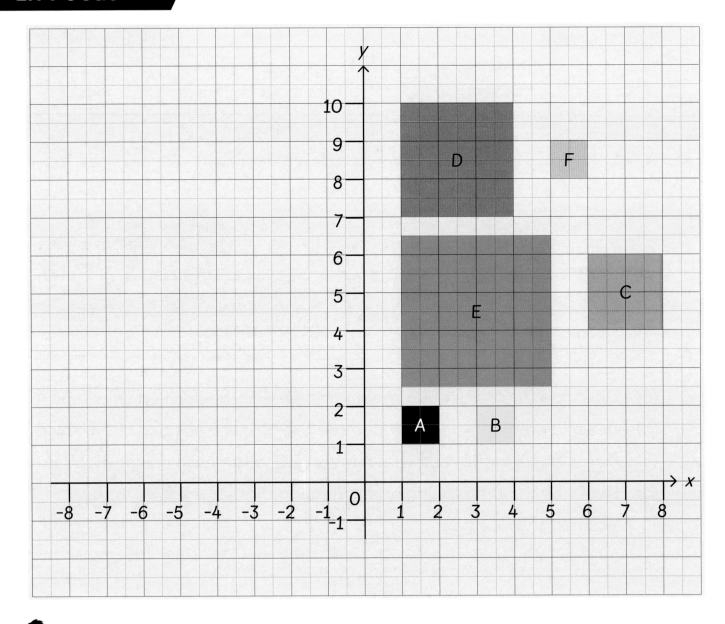

drew squares on the coordinate grid. Given the coordinates of a square's vertex, is it possible to work out the coordinates of the opposite vertex?

1 Complete the table and observe a pattern.

square	coordinates of opposite vertices	
■	(1, 1) and (2, 2)	(2, ⬜) and (1, ⬜)
⬜	(3, 1) and (4, 2)	(4, ⬜) and (3, ⬜)
⬜	(5, 8) and (6, 9)	(6, ⬜) and (5, ⬜)

(1, 1) and (2, 2)
(3, 1) and (4, 2)
(5, 8) and (6, 9)

(x, y) and (⬜ , ⬜)

(2, 1) and (1, 2)
(4, 1) and (3, 2)
(6, 8) and (5, 9)

(p, q) and (⬜ , ⬜)

For 1 by 1 squares drawn this way, the coordinates of the opposite vertices are:

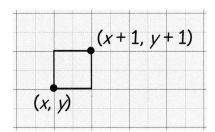

(x + 1, y + 1)

(x, y)

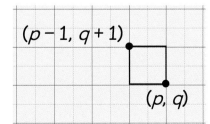

(p − 1, q + 1)

(p, q)

2 Complete the table and observe a pattern.

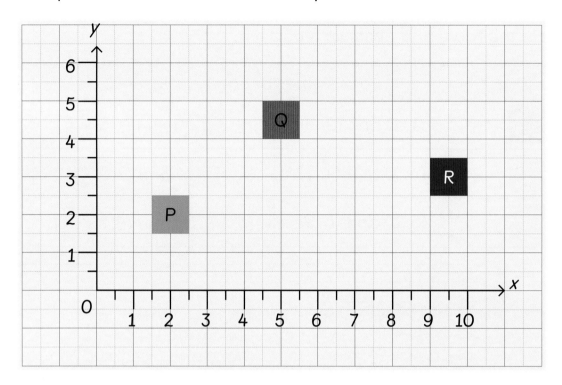

square	coordinates of opposite vertices	
P	$(1\frac{1}{2}, 1\frac{1}{2})$ and $(2\frac{1}{2}, 2\frac{1}{2})$	$(2\frac{1}{2}, 1\frac{1}{2})$ and $(1\frac{1}{2}, 2\frac{1}{2})$
Q	$(4\frac{1}{2}, 4)$ and $(5\frac{1}{2}, 5)$	$(5\frac{1}{2}, 4)$ and $(4\frac{1}{2}, 5)$
R	$(\ \boxed{}\ , 2\frac{1}{2})$ and $(\ \boxed{}\ , 3\frac{1}{2})$	$(10, \boxed{})$ and $(9, \boxed{})$
S	(x, y) and $(\ \boxed{}\ , \boxed{}\ )$	(p, q) and $(\ \boxed{}\ , \boxed{}\ )$

For squares drawn this way, the coordinates of the opposite vertices are:

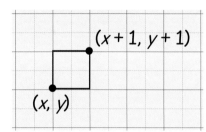 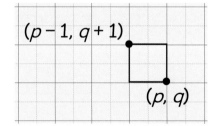

3 Complete the table and observe a pattern.

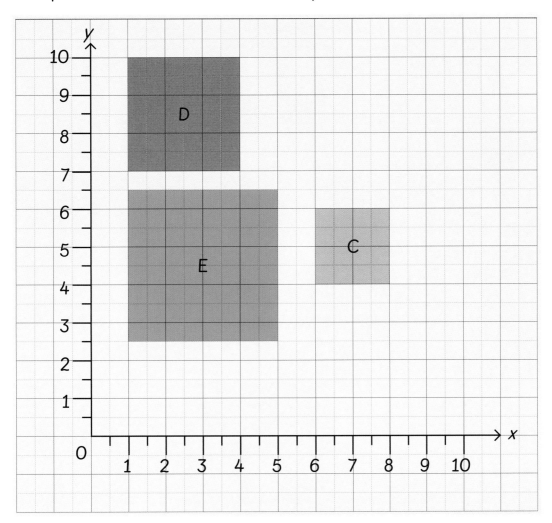

square	coordinates of opposite vertices	
▩	(6, 4) and (8, 6)	(8, 4) and (6, 6)
▩	(1 , 7) and (4 , 10)	(4, 7) and (1, 10)
▩	(1 , $2\frac{1}{2}$) and (5 , $6\frac{1}{2}$)	(5, $2\frac{1}{2}$) and (1, $6\frac{1}{2}$)

Is there a pattern?

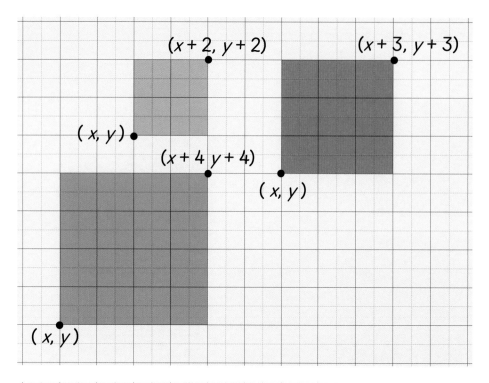

$(x + 2, y + 2)$

$(x + 3, y + 3)$

(x, y)

$(x + 4, y + 4)$

(x, y)

(x, y)

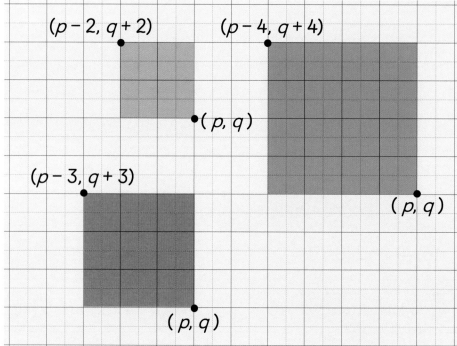

$(p - 2, q + 2)$

$(p - 4, q + 4)$

(p, q)

$(p - 3, q + 3)$

(p, q)

(p, q)

Is there a pattern?

1 The sides of the square are 2 units.

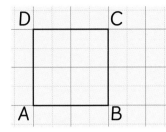

A is (a, b).

Find the coordinates of the other three vertices.

2 The sides of the rectangle are 1 unit and 3 units.

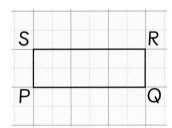

P is (x, y).

Find the coordinates of the other three vertices.

3

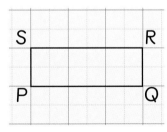

D is (5, t).

Find the coordinates of the other three vertices.

4

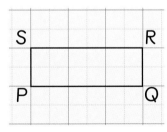

R is (m, n).

Find the coordinates of the other three vertices.

Complete Worksheet 9 – Page 144 – 145

Using Algebra to Describe Movements

In Focus

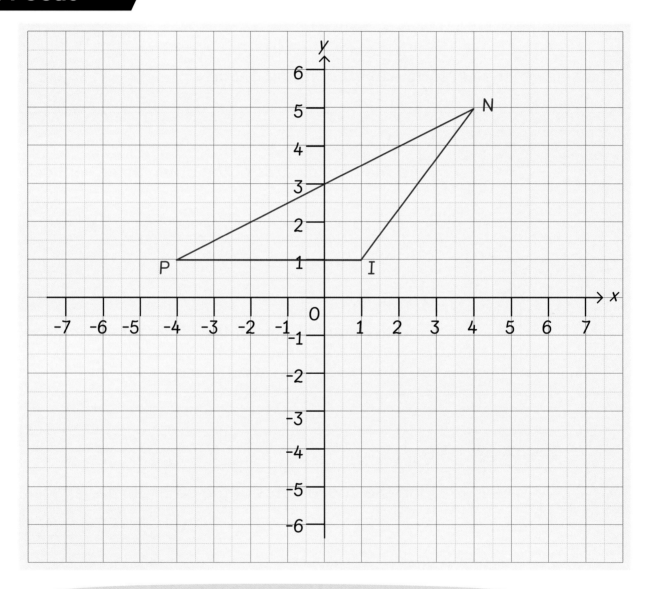

When the triangle is translated or reflected, we can tell the coordinates of the new position by looking at the coordinates of the original position.

Is this true?

1 The triangle is reflected in the *y*-axis.

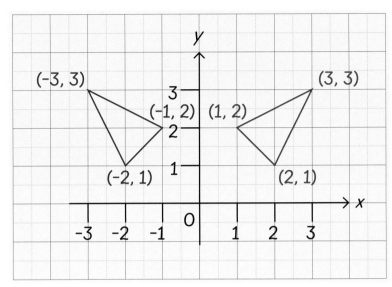

$(3, 3) \longrightarrow (-3, 3)$

$(2, 1) \longrightarrow (-2, 1)$

$(1, 2) \longrightarrow (-1, 2)$

What do you notice?

$(a, b) \longrightarrow ($ ⬜ , ⬜ $)$

2 The triangle is reflected in the *x*-axis.

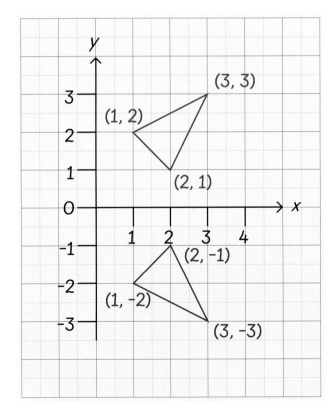

$(3, 3) \longrightarrow (3, -3)$

$(2, 1) \longrightarrow (2, -1)$

$(1, 2) \longrightarrow (1, -2)$

What do you notice?

$(a, b) \longrightarrow ($ ⬜ , ⬜ $)$

3 The triangle is translated 1 unit upwards and 4 units to the right.

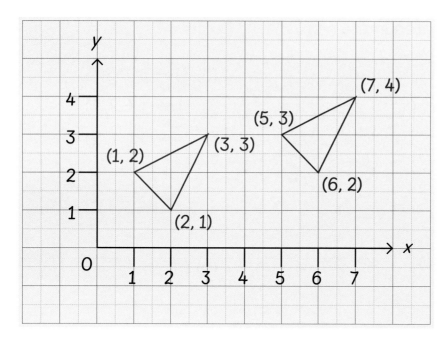

$(3, 3) \longrightarrow (7, 4)$

$(2, 1) \longrightarrow (6, 2)$

$(1, 2) \longrightarrow (5, 3)$

$(a, b) \longrightarrow ($ ▢ , ▢ $)$

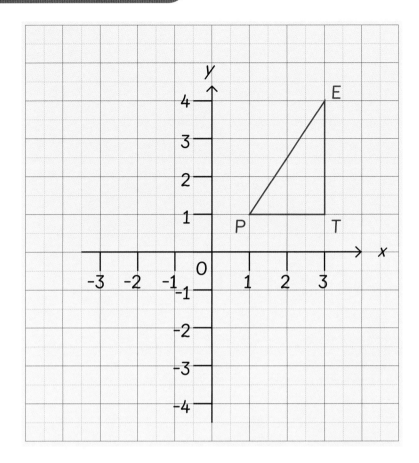

1 Triangle PET is reflected in the *x*-axis.

(a) The image of point P(1, 1) is (,   ).

(b) The image of any point (*x, y*) on the triangle is (,   ).

2 Triangle PET is reflected in the *y*-axis.

(a) The image of point E(3, 4) is (,   ).

(b) The image of any point (*x, y*) on the triangle is (,   ).

3 Triangle PET is translated 4 units to the left and 2 units downwards.

(a) The image of point T(3, 1) is (,   ).

(b) The image of any point (*x, y*) on the triangle is (,   ).

Complete Worksheet **10** – Page **146 – 147**

Mind Workout

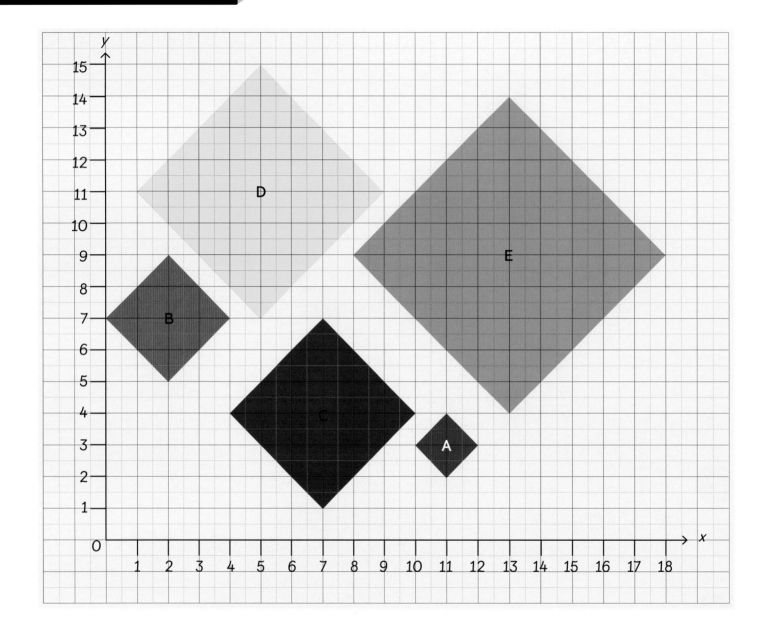

Square	Area (unit²)	Coordinates of four vertices			
A					
B					
C					
D					
E					

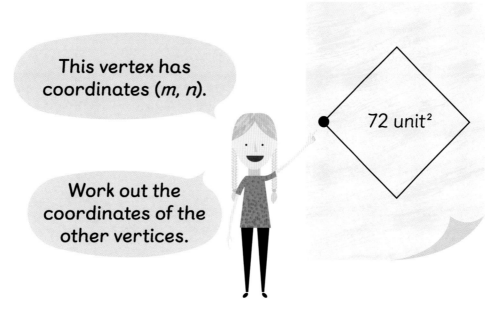

This vertex has coordinates (*m, n*).

Work out the coordinates of the other vertices.

72 unit²

Triangle PIN is isosceles.

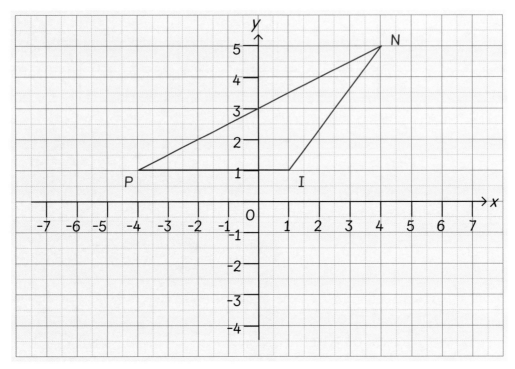

1 Find a different position for P so that the triangle PIN is still an isosceles triangle. Explain how this is possible.

2 Find different positions for K so that the quadrilateral PINK is a trapezium. Explain how this is possible.

3 Is it possible for quadrilateral PINK to be a rhombus? Explain.

I know how to...

☐ use coordinate grids with negative numbers.

☐ describe positions of points using coordinates.

☐ draw, translate and reflect simple shapes on the coordinate plane.

Self Check

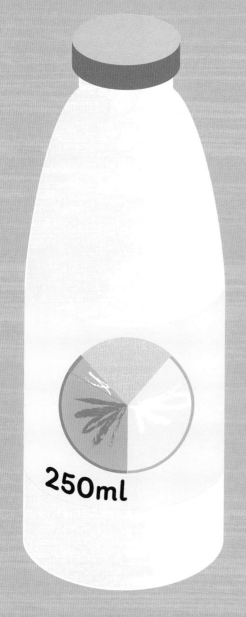

Chapter 14
Graphs and Averages

Understanding Averages

In Focus

The picture shows how many pizza slices each child ate for lunch.

How much pizza is that per child?

How can you answer this question by giving just one number?

1 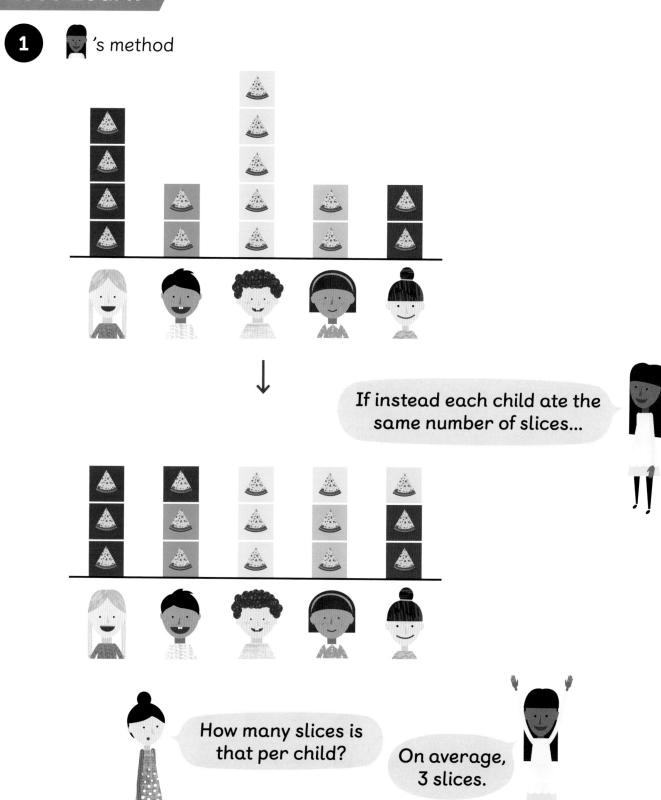's method

If instead each child ate the same number of slices...

How many slices is that per child?

On average, 3 slices.

2  's method

How many slices did each child eat?

I say 2 slices per child.

Number of slices	Number of people
2	
4	
5	

Why did  say 2 slices per child?

3 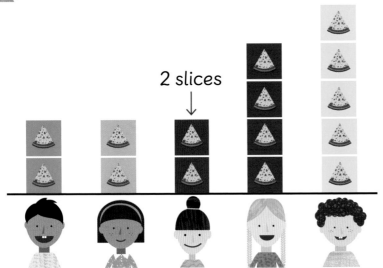 's method

2 slices

How many slices did each child eat?

I also say 2 slices per child...

but I have a different reason.

Why did  say 2 slices per child?

My method shares the total as if each child ate the same number of slices. On average, each child ate 3 slices.

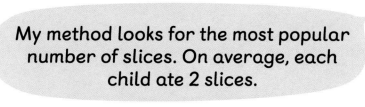

My method looks for the most popular number of slices. On average, each child ate 2 slices.

I say the average is 2 slices because 2 is in the middle: two children ate 2 or fewer slices, and two children ate 2 or more slices, than Emma.

There are different ways to calculate average.

Guided Practice

1 The picture graph shows children in three groups.

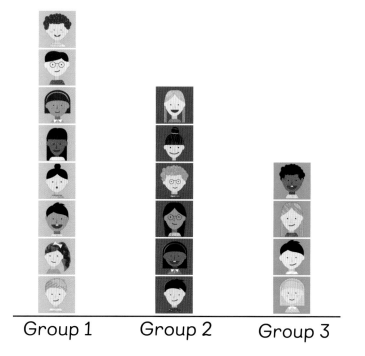

Group 1   Group 2   Group 3

Use my method.

On average, how many children are there in each group?

2 The bar graph shows the number of cupcakes four friends bought at a bakery.

number of cupcakes bought

Use my method.

On average, how many cupcakes did each of them buy?

3 The graph shows how much 👧 spent over five days.

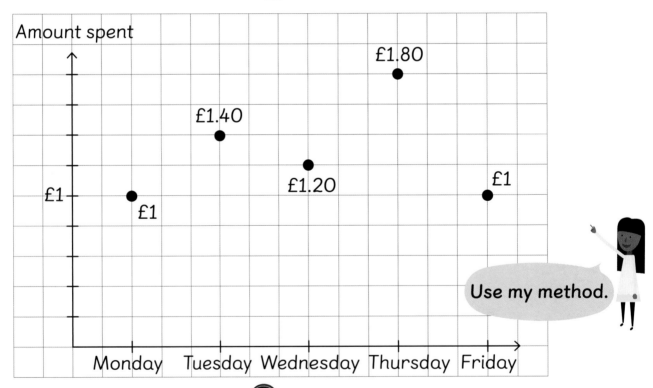

Amount spent

£1.80

£1.40

£1.20

£1

£1

£1

Monday   Tuesday Wednesday Thursday Friday

Use my method.

On average, how much did 👧 spend each day?

Complete Worksheet **1** – Page **153 – 154**

Calculating the Mean

In Focus

Here is a chart of the number of goals scored in a football tournament.

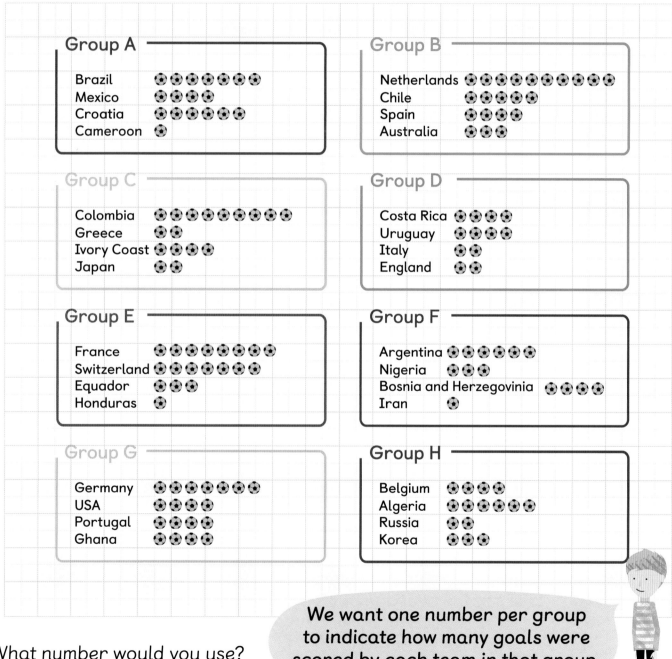

Group A
Brazil
Mexico
Croatia
Cameroon

Group B
Netherlands
Chile
Spain
Australia

Group C
Colombia
Greece
Ivory Coast
Japan

Group D
Costa Rica
Uruguay
Italy
England

Group E
France
Switzerland
Equador
Honduras

Group F
Argentina
Nigeria
Bosnia and Herzegovinia
Iran

Group G
Germany
USA
Portugal
Ghana

Group H
Belgium
Algeria
Russia
Korea

We want one number per group to indicate how many goals were scored by each team in that group.

What number would you use?

1 Group D

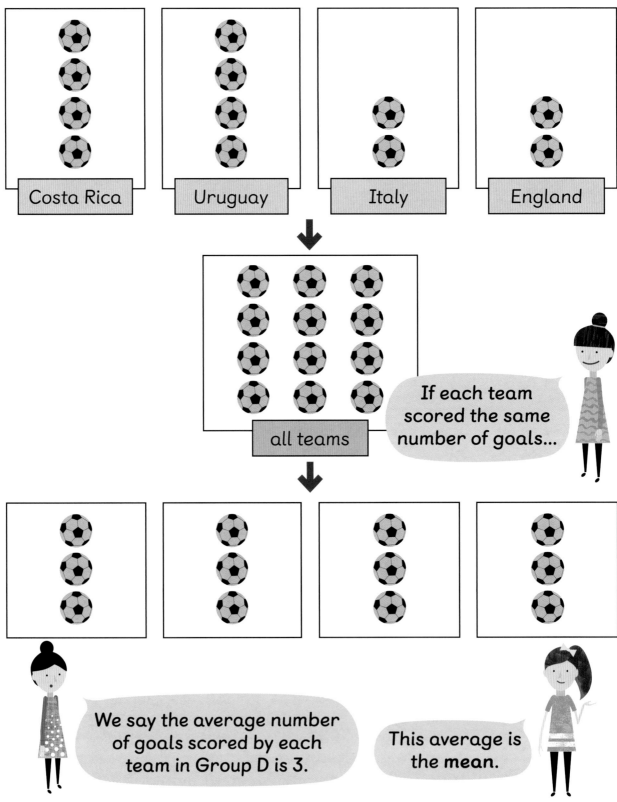

Costa Rica   Uruguay   Italy   England

all teams

If each team scored the same number of goals...

We say the average number of goals scored by each team in Group D is 3.

This average is the mean.

Did each team really score 3 goals?

2 Group C

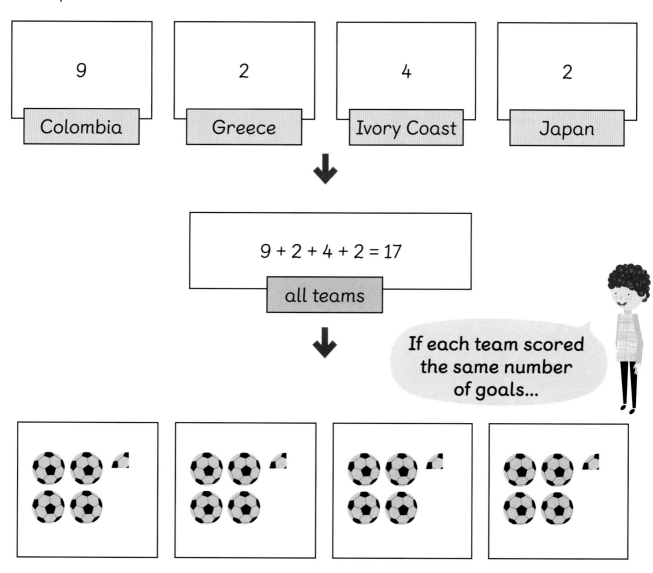

9	2	4	2
Colombia	Greece	Ivory Coast	Japan

9 + 2 + 4 + 2 = 17

all teams

If each team scored the same number of goals...

On average, each team in Group C scored $4\frac{1}{4}$ goals.

Mean = $4\frac{1}{4}$

Did each team really score $4\frac{1}{4}$ goals?

1

Group F

	number of goals over three matches
Argentina	6
Nigeria	3
Bosnia and Herzegovina	4
Iran	1

Calculate the mean number of goals scored per match:

(a) by Argentina

(b) by Nigeria

(c) by Bosnia and Herzegovina

(d) by Iran

2 The mean number of goals scored over three matches for the teams in one group was 4.5. Which group was this?

Group A

	number of goals
Brazil	7
Croatia	6
Mexico	4
Cameroon	1

Group B

	number of goals
Netherlands	10
Chile	5
Spain	4
Australia	3

Group E

	number of goals
France	8
Switzerland	7
Ecuador	3
Honduras	1

Complete Worksheet 2 – Page 155 – 156

Calculating the Mean

In Focus

The mean age of a group of five people is 12 years old.
How old is each person in this group?

Mean age = 12 years old

Let's Learn

1 Find the mean age.

12 years   12 years   12 years   12 years   12 years

mean = 12 years

9 + 10 + 12 + 14 + 15 = 60

2

9 years   10 years   12 years   14 years   15 years

mean = 60 ÷ 5
     = 12 years

3

   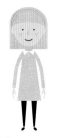 

8 years 10 years 13 years 14 years 15 years

$8 + 10 + 13 + 14 + 15 = 60$

mean = $60 \div 5$

= 12 years

4

5 years 7 years 8 years 10 years 30 years

$5 + 7 + 8 + 10 + 30 = 60$

mean = $60 \div 5$

= 12 years

5

50 years 2 years 2 years 3 years 3 years

$50 + 2 + 3 + 2 + 3 = 60$

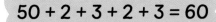

mean = $60 \div 5$

= 12 years

Do you think the mean age is a good indicator of how old the five people are?

1 Calculate the mean age of each group.

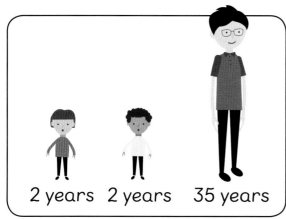

2 years 2 years 35 years

12 years 12 years 11 years 13 years

Is the mean a good indicator of how old the people in each group are?

2 The mean height of three people is 170 cm.

(a) Is it possible that all three people are 170 cm tall?

(b) Is it possible for exactly one of them to be 170 cm tall?

(c) Is it possible for exactly two of them to be 170 cm tall?

(d) Is it possible for none of them to be 170 cm tall?

Explain each answer by giving an example.

Complete Worksheet **3** – Page **157 – 158**

Solving Problems Involving the Mean

In Focus

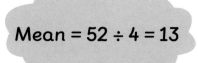 played 6 games during a basketball tournament. After 4 games, her mean score per game was 13 points. For all 6 games, her mean score per game was 14 points.

How many points did she score in the last two games?

Let's Learn

1 The mean score for 4 games was 13.

Total score for 4 games = 13 × 4

= 52 points

Mean = 52 ÷ 4 = 13

2 The mean score for 6 games was 14.

Total score for 6 games = 14 × 6

= 84 points

3 Find 's score for the last two games.

total for 4 games	52	?

total for 6 games	84

84 − 52 = 32

 scored a total of 32 points in the last two games.

Can you work out her score in the final game?

$x + y = 32$

Guided Practice

1 The mean age of four siblings is 7 years old.
The mean age of the youngest three is 5 years old.
How old is the eldest sibling?

What is the total age of the four siblings?

What is the total age of the three younger siblings?

2

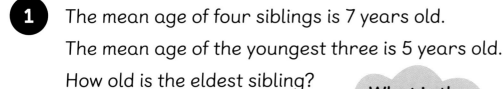

Test 1	70
Test 2	76
Test 3	7
Test 4	8
Test 5	8

's scores for 5 tests are all different and they are arranged from lowest to highest. Three of the unit digits are missing. Find the lowest possible value for 's score in Test 3.

The mean of my test scores is 79 points.

Test scores are in whole numbers.

Complete Worksheet **4** – Page **159 – 160**

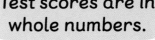

Showing Information on Graphs

In Focus

24 children voted on the colour of their class T-shirt.

How can we show this information?

1  's method

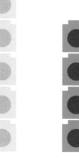

2 's method

T-shirt Colours

blue	red	yellow	green
12	2	6	4

I use a table.

3  's method

☺ stands for 2 children.

4  's method

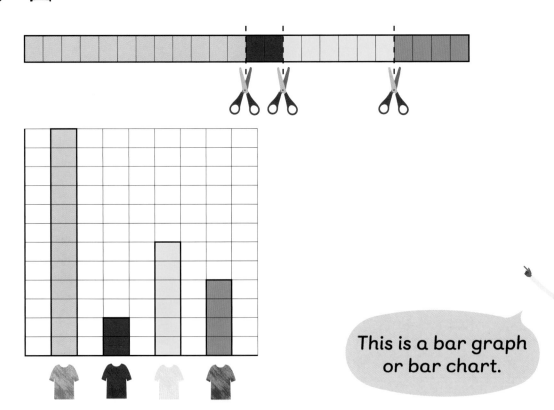

This is a picture graph or a pictogram.

This is a bar graph or bar chart.

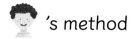

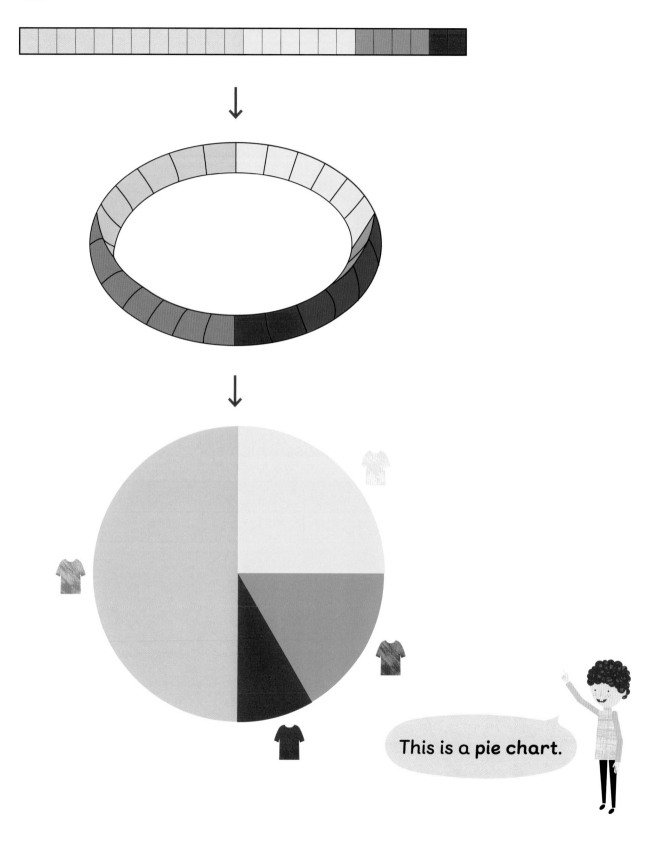

This is a pie chart.

1 The table shows how a group of 48 pupils travel to school.

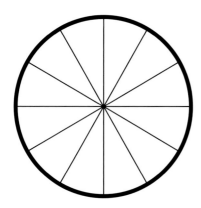				others
24	4	8	12	0

Show the information on a pie chart.

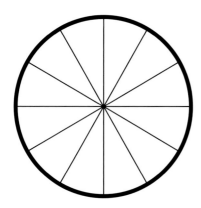

2 60 children at a sports camp choose which sport to play.

football	basketball	badminton	hockey	rugby
20	15	10	10	5

Show the information on a pie chart.

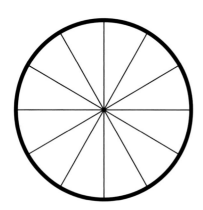

Complete Worksheet 5 – Page 161 – 162

Reading Pie Charts

In Focus

A group of people picked
their favourite pizza toppings
from a list of four. Is there
enough information on the
pie chart to complete the table?

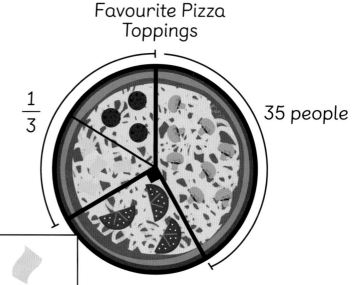

Favourite Pizza
Toppings

$\frac{1}{3}$

35 people

Let's Learn

1 What fraction of the group chose mushrooms?

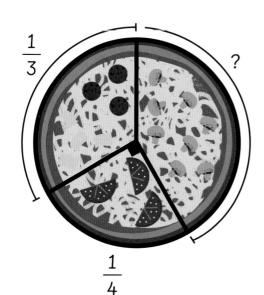

$\frac{1}{3}$

?

$\frac{1}{4}$

$\dfrac{1}{3} + \dfrac{1}{4} = \dfrac{4}{12} + \dfrac{3}{12}$

$= \dfrac{7}{12}$

$1 - \dfrac{7}{12} = \dfrac{12}{12} - \dfrac{7}{12}$

$= \dfrac{5}{12}$

Graphs and Averages   Page 233

2 Complete the table.

Toppings	🍄	🍕	⬤ 〰
Number of people			

$$\frac{5}{12} \qquad \frac{1}{4} \qquad \frac{1}{3}$$

$\dfrac{5}{12} \longrightarrow 35$ people

$\dfrac{1}{12} \longrightarrow 35 \div 5 = 7$ people

$\dfrac{1}{4} = \dfrac{3}{12} \longrightarrow 3 \times 7$ people = ☐

$\dfrac{1}{3} = \dfrac{4}{12} \longrightarrow 4 \times 7$ people = ☐

Can we assume 14 people chose ham and 14 people chose pepperoni?

Guided Practice

1 The following table and pie chart show the number of goals scored by 32 teams in a football tournament.

Number of goals scored	Number of teams
1 or 2	x
3 or 4	14
5 or 6	y
7 or 8	4
9 or 10	z

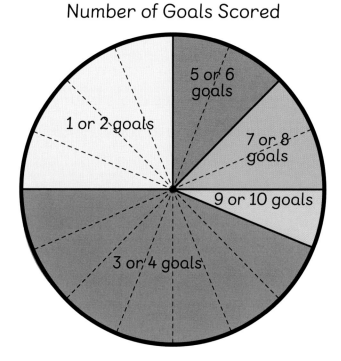

Number of Goals Scored

Find the values of x, y and z.

2

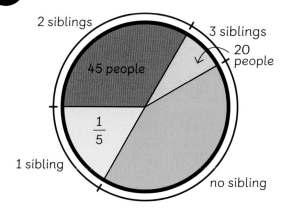

2 siblings

3 siblings
20 people

45 people

$\frac{1}{5}$

1 sibling

no sibling

did a survey among his classmates. He found that:

- $\frac{1}{5}$ of those he surveyed have one sibling
- 45 of those he surveyed have two siblings
- 20 of those he surveyed have three siblings
- none of them has more than three siblings

Complete the table.

Number of siblings	0	1	2	3
Number of people			45	20

Complete Worksheet **6** – Page **163 – 164**

Reading Pie Charts

In Focus

A fruit juice maker uses a pie chart to describe the contents of its fruit juice. Describe the contents using lengths of pieces of fruit.

banana 20%

lime

orange 32%

40%

pineapple

250ml

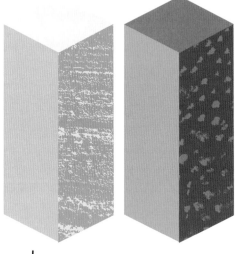

banana   orange   pineapple   lime

If the pineapple column is 5 cm tall, how tall should the other columns be?

Let's Learn

1 What percent of the fruit juice is lime?

$x\%$

20%

32%

40%

$20 + 40 + 32 = 92$

$100 - 92 = 8$

8% of the fruit juice is lime.

$x = 8$

2 Calculate the height of the rectangles in the bar chart.

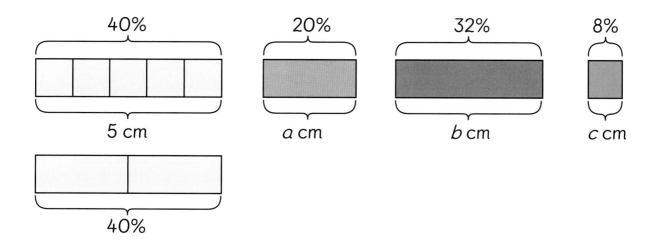

40% → 5 cm
20% → 2.5 cm
a = 2.5

5 ÷ 2 = ☐

40% → 5 cm
32% → 4 cm
b = 4

40% → 5 cm
8% → 1 cm
16% → 2 cm
32% → 4 cm

40% → 5 cm
8% → 1 cm
c = 1

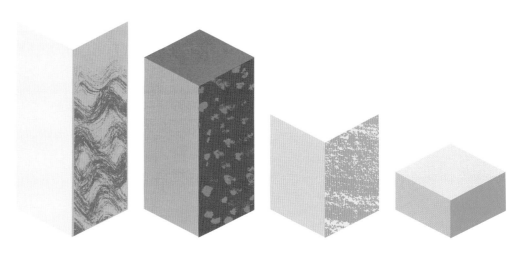

3 Calculate the volume of each type of fruit juice in a bottle.

250ml

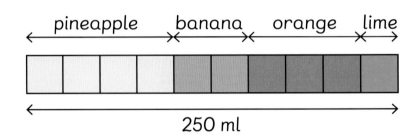

pineapple   banana   orange   lime

250 ml

Volume of pineapple juice = 40% × 250 ml

= 250 ÷ 10 × 4

= 25 × 4

= 100 ml

Volume of banana juice = 20% × 250 ml

= 250 ÷ 10 × 2

= 25 × 2

= 50 ml

> Alternatively,
> 40% → 100 ml
> 20% → 50 ml

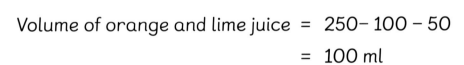

Volume of orange and lime juice = 250 – 100 – 50

= 100 ml

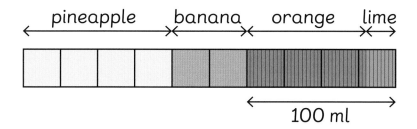

Volume of orange juice $= 100 \div 40 \times 32$
$= 2.5 \times 32$
$= 80$ ml

Volume of lime juice $= 100 \div 40 \times 8$
$= 2.5 \times 8$
$= 20$ ml

Alternatively,

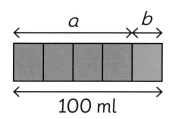

$a = 100 \div 5 \times 4$
$= 20 \times 4$
$= 80$ ml
$b = 100 \div 5$
$= 20$ ml

$a : b$
$= 80$ ml $: 20$ml
$= \quad 4 : 1$

1

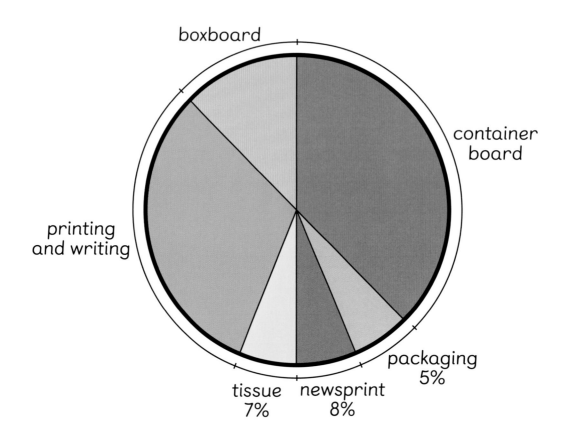

boxboard

container
board

printing
and writing

packaging
5%

tissue
7%

newsprint
8%

Uses of Paper and Cardboard

The pie chart shows how paper is used in a country in a particular year.

What percentage is used for the following?

(a) boxboard

(b) container board

(c) printing and writing

2 The pie chart shows the percentage of pupils who ordered T-shirts of different sizes.

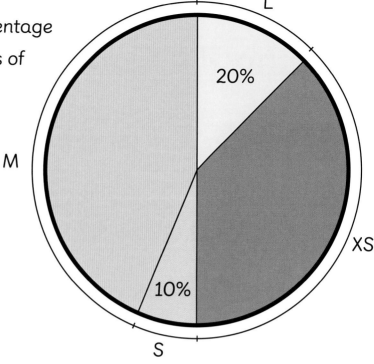

T-shirt Sizes

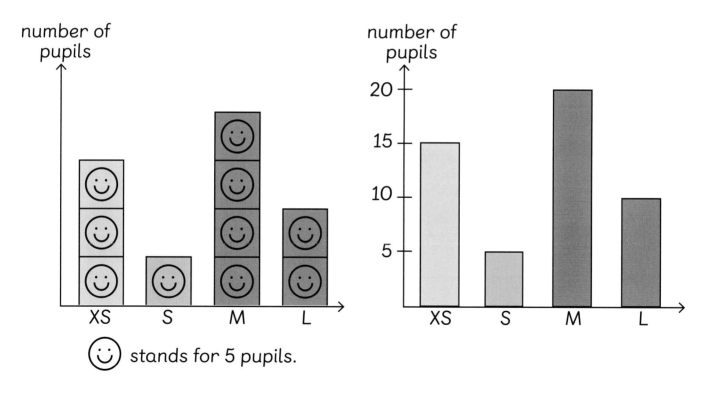

☺ stands for 5 pupils.

Do these two graphs show the same information?

Complete Worksheet **7** – Page **165 – 166**

Reading Pie Charts

In Focus

Average Daily Spending by
European Tourists in Thailand

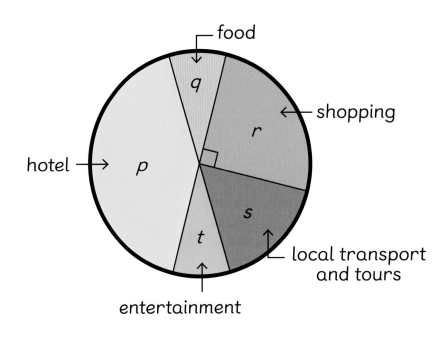

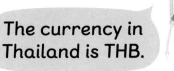

The currency in
Thailand is THB.

Which amounts do you need to know in order to work out the other amounts?

1 The average amount spent on food each day is THB650.

q = THB650

If the value of q is given, we can find the value of t.

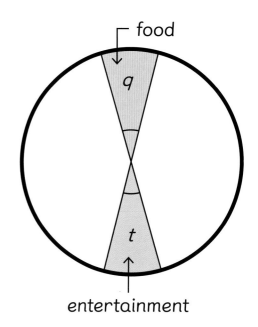

food

q

t

entertainment

2 The average daily amount spent on shopping is THB1500.

r = THB1500

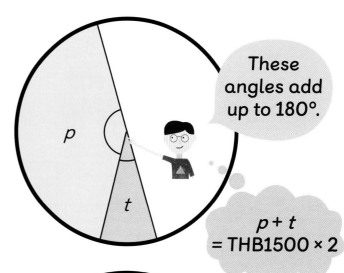

p

t

These angles add up to 180°.

$p + t$
= THB1500 × 2

If the value of r is given, we can find the value of $p + t$ or $q + s$.

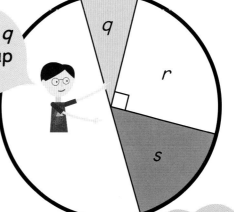

q

r

s

The angles q and s add up to 90°.

We can also find the total value of $p + q + r + s + t$.

$q + s$ = THB1500

3 Suppose we know that
q = THB650 and r = THB1500.

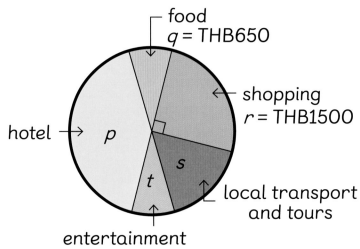

food
q = THB650

shopping
r = THB1500

hotel →

p

s

t

local transport
and tours

entertainment

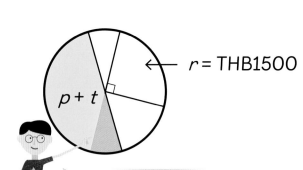

r = THB1500

$p + t$

$p + t = 2 \times$ THB1500
$p + t =$ THB3000

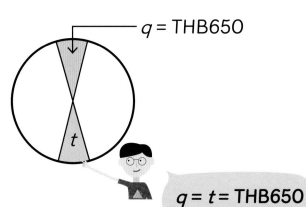

q = THB650

t

$q = t =$ THB650

$p + t =$ THB3000

$t =$ THB650

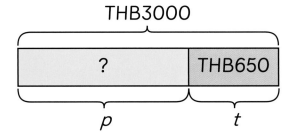

THB3000

?

THB650

p

t

p = THB3000 – THB650

= THB2350

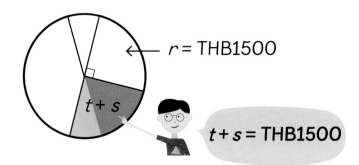

r = THB1500

$t + s$

$t + s =$ THB1500

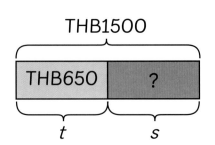

THB1500

THB650

?

t

s

s = THB1500 – THB650

=

1 The pie chart shows the votes for the
   five finalists in a talent competition.
   The winner received 3000 votes.

   (a) Find the number of votes received
        by the other finalists.

   (b) Find the total number of votes.

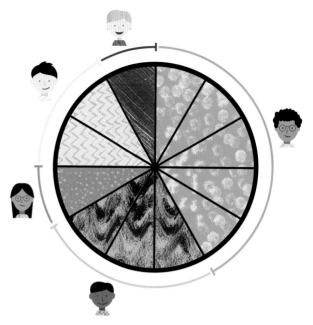

Votes for Finalists

2 The pie chart shows the favourite field trip of $a + b + c + x$ pupils.

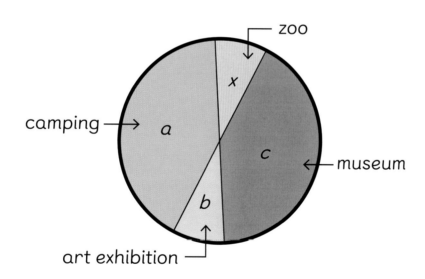

Favourite Field Trip

   (a) Given that $x = 4$, explain if it is possible to find the values of a, b and c.

   (b) What information is available from the pie chart?

Complete Worksheet 8 – Page **167 – 168**

Reading Line Graphs

In Focus

 has a device that tells him how far and how long he has been walking or running. He took the readings every 10 minutes during a walk.

time in min	10	20	30	40	50
distance walked in km	1	2	3	4	5

Draw a graph to show these readings.
Did speed up or slow down during the walk?

Let's Learn

1 drew a line graph.

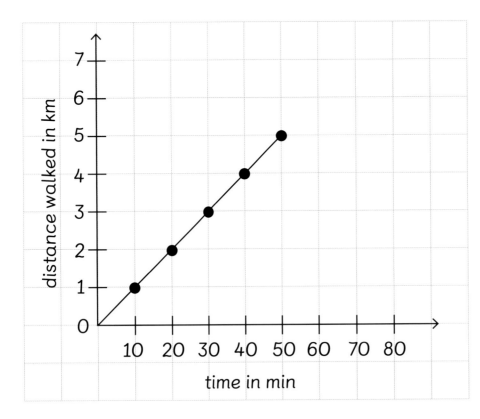

I walked 1 km every 10 minutes. I did not speed up or slow down. My speed did not change.

2 How far could walk in 1 hour at this speed?

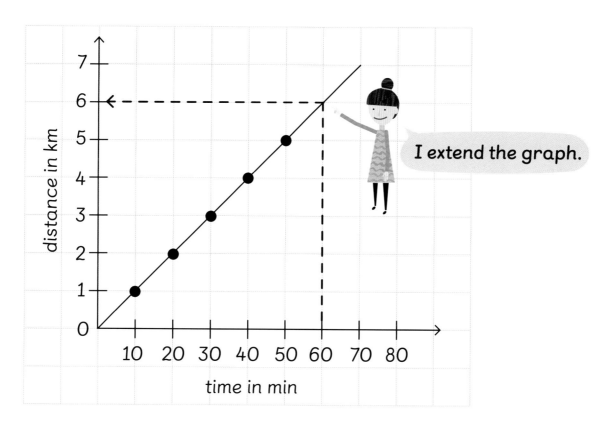

I extend the graph.

At this speed, could walk 6 km in 1 hour.

We can say my walking speed was 6 km per hour.

The graph shows the distance a train travelled between two cities, X and Y.

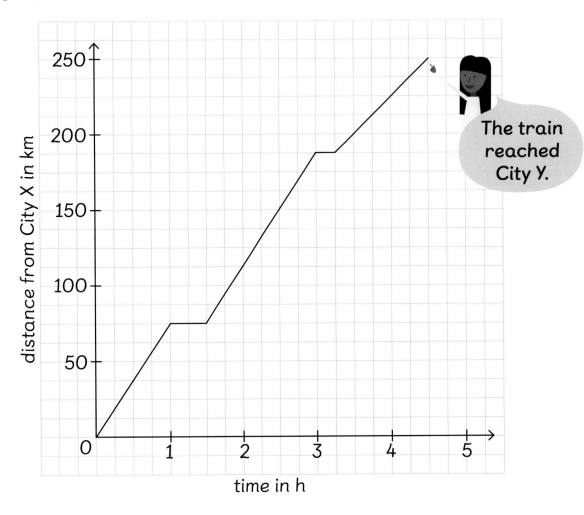

The train reached City Y.

1. (a) How far was the train from City X after 3 h?

   (b) How far was the train from City Y after 3 h?

2. (a) How many times did the train stop during the journey between City X and City Y?

   (b) How long was each stop?

3. How long was the entire journey including the stops?

What other questions can we answer using information from the graph?

Complete Worksheet **9** – Page **169 – 170**

Reading Line Graphs

In Focus

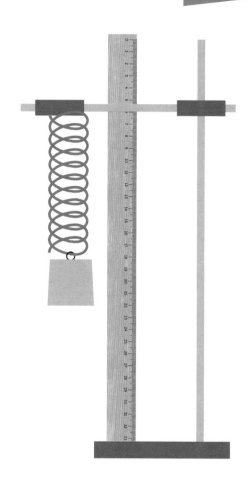 did an experiment to investigate how the length of a spring changes when weights are added to it.

The results are recorded in a table.

weights added in g	0	20	40	60	80	100
ruler reading in cm	20.1	20.6	21.1	21.8	22.1	22.6

Show the results on a graph. How does the graph suggest that 👧 may have made a mistake during the experiment?

drew a line graph.

weights added, w, in g	0	20	40	60	80	100
ruler reading in cm	20.1	20.6	21.1	21.8	22.1	22.6
extension of the spring, x, in cm	0	0.5	1.0	1.7	2.0	2.5

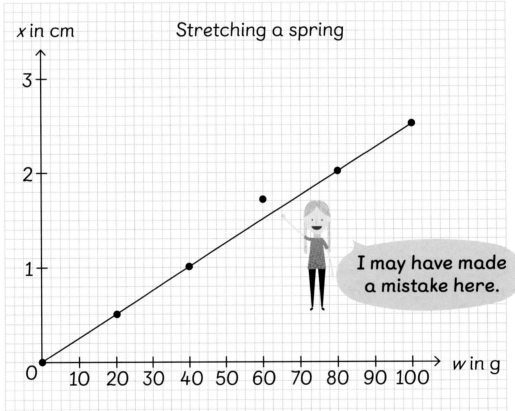

I may have made a mistake here.

The graph suggests that when 60 g is added, the extension should be 1.5 cm instead of 1.7 cm.

I can also predict the extension for other weights.

The graph shows wages paid to teenagers by a fast-food restaurant.

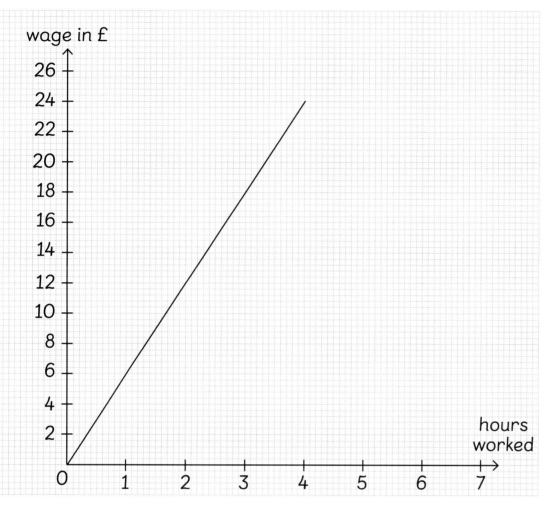

1 worked for 4 h. Find his wage.

2 worked for $4\frac{1}{2}$ h. Find her wage.

3 worked for 7 h. Find his wage.

4 earned £21 on Monday evening.

Find the number of hours he worked that evening.

Complete Worksheet 10 – Page 171 - 172

Converting Miles into Kilometres

In Focus

 uses 1 mile = 1.6 km to find out the distance

between two places. uses 1 mile = 1.609 km.

Does it make much difference?

150 miles

Do you know two places that are 150 miles apart?

Let's Learn

1   Take 1 mile = 1.6 km.

$$1 \text{ mile} = 1.6 \text{ km}$$
$$10 \text{ miles} = 16 \text{ km}$$
$$100 \text{ miles} = 160 \text{ km}$$

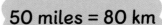

50 miles = 80 km

 I get 150 miles = 160 km + 80 km

  = 240 km

2   Take 1 mile = 1.609 km.

$$1 \text{ mile} = 1.609 \text{ km}$$
$$10 \text{ miles} = 16.09 \text{ km}$$
$$100 \text{ miles} = 160.9 \text{ km}$$

50 miles = (160.9 ÷ 2) km

 I get 150 miles = 160.9 km + 80.45 km

  = 241.35 km

Guided Practice

1 My home is 5 km from my grandparents' house.

That's about 2 miles.

No, it's about 3 miles.

1 mile is approximately 1.6 km.

I think it's closer to 4 miles.

Isn't 5 km about 5 miles?

Who gives the best estimate?

2 On a website, found the distance from London to several places.

(a) London is about 60 miles from Whitstable in Kent.

60 miles = ___ km (to the nearest km)

(b) London is 350 km from Paris.

350 km = ___ miles (to the nearest 10 miles)

(c) London is 6740 miles from Singapore.

6740 miles = ___ km (to the nearest 10 km)

Complete Worksheet **11** – Page **173 - 174**

Reading Line Graphs

In Focus

This graph shows how distances in kilometres and miles are related.

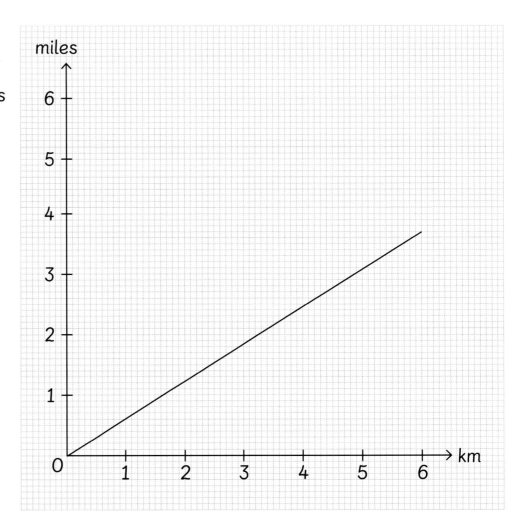

Use the diagrams and the graph to describe how far each town is from another, in miles and in kilometres.

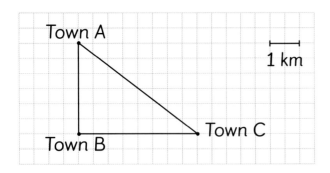

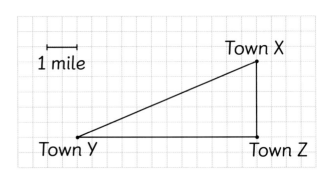

1

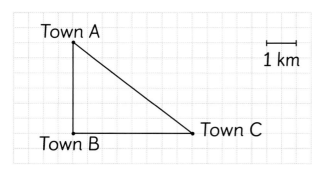

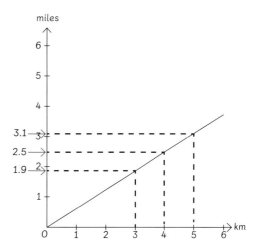

distance between	in km	in miles
Town A and Town B	3	≈
Town B and Town C	4	≈
Town C and Town A	5	≈

3 km is approximately 1.9 miles.

2

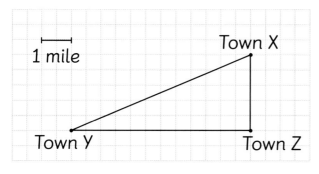

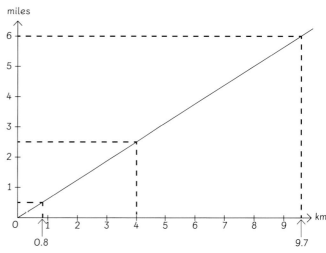

distance between	in miles	in km
Town Y and Town Z	6	≈
Town Z and Town X	2.5	≈
Town X and Town Y	6.5	≈

6.5 miles ≈ 10.5 km

6 miles ≈ 9.7 km

0.5 miles ≈ 0.8 km

Guided Practice

This graph shows how the British pound is related to the Singapore dollar (SGD) and the US dollar (USD).

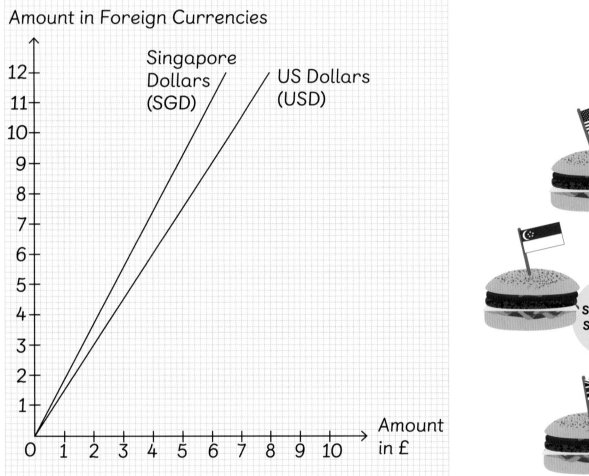

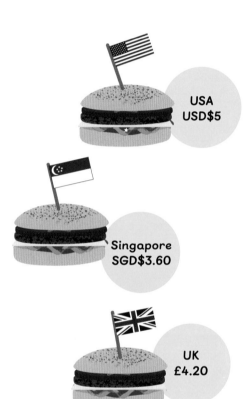

1 (a) How much, in £, does the burger cost in the US?

(b) How much, in £, does the burger cost in Singapore?

2 (a) A tourist from the US buys a 🍔 £4.20.
How much does it cost her in USD?

(b) A tourist from Singapore buys a 🍔 £4.20.
How much does it cost him in SGD?

Complete Worksheet **12** – Page **175**

Our average mass is 50 kg.

100 kg

Four children weigh themselves in pairs and take the average mass of each pair. The average mass of the six pairs are:

47 kg,   50 kg,   51 kg,   53 kg,   54 kg,   57 kg

Find the mass of the heaviest child.

Maths Journal

A class of 24 in England and a class of 36 in Singapore chose the colour of their class T-shirts.

England	12	2	6	4
Singapore	12	9	6	9

I drew these pie charts.

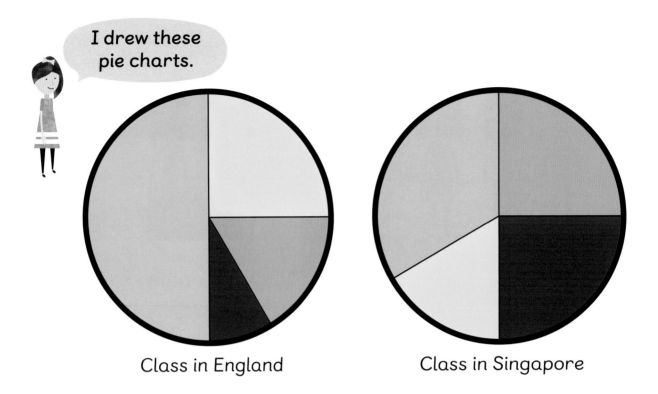

Class in England   Class in Singapore

Explain how to draw the pie chart for the class in Singapore.

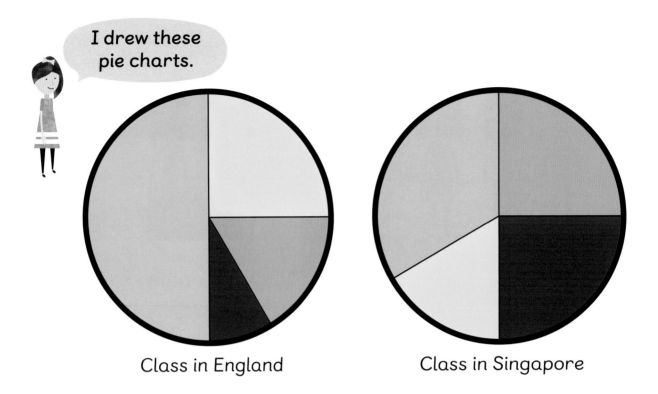 used the same radius for both pie charts. Why are 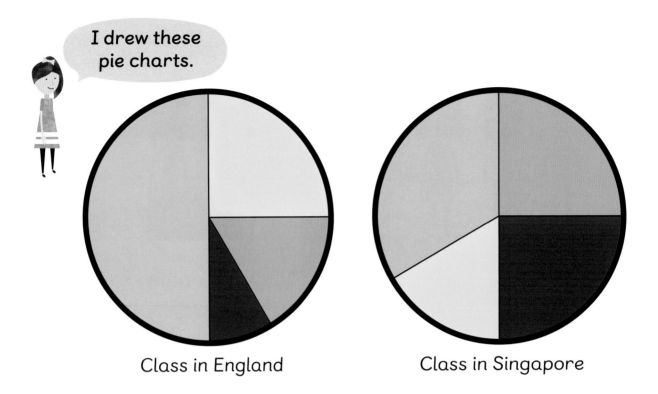 's pie charts

misleading?

I know how to...

☐ calculate and interpret the mean as an average.

☐ draw and read pie charts.

☐ draw and read graphs.

☐ solve problems using information provided by graphs.

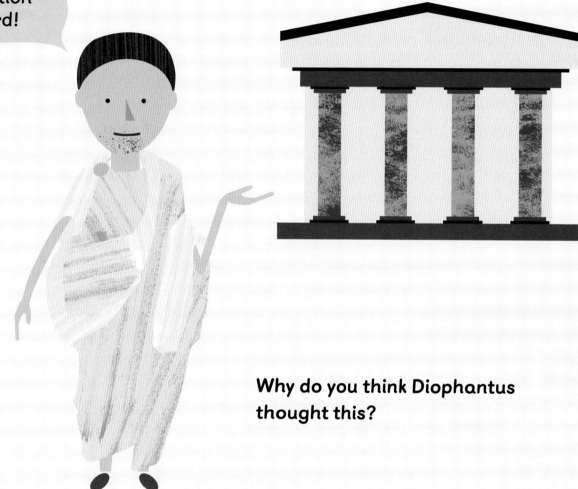

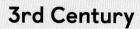

3rd Century

$$4x + 20 = 4$$

The equation is absurd!

Why do you think Diophantus thought this?

Chapter 15
Negative Numbers

Adding and Subtracting Negative Numbers

In Focus

 uses this method to add and subtract numbers.

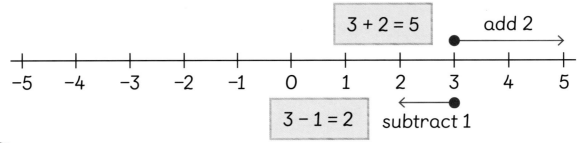

$3 + 2 = 5$ add 2

$3 - 1 = 2$ subtract 1

Use 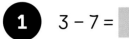's method to calculate the values of $3 - 7$ and $-4 + 3$.

Let's Learn

1 $3 - 7 =$ ▢

subtract 7

$3 - 7 = -4$

We read -4 as 'negative four'.

-4 is 4 less than 0.

2 $-4 + 3 =$ ▢

add 3

$-4 + 3 = -1$

We read -1 as 'negative one'.

-1 is 1 less than 0.

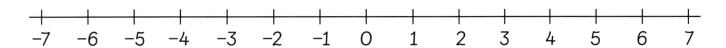

1 Calculate the value of each of the following.

(a) $3 + 1 =$ ☐

(b) $-3 - 1 =$ ☐

(c) $-3 + 1 =$ ☐

(d) $3 - 1 =$ ☐

2 Find the value of each of the following.

(a) $-2 + 1$

(b) $-2 + 5$

(c) $-2 - 5$

3 ⬤ + ▲ = -3

(a) ⬤ is a negative number. What numbers could ⬤ and ▲ be?

(b) ▲ is a positive number. What numbers could ⬤ and ▲ be?

Complete Worksheet 1 – Page 181 – 182 ▶

Using Negative Numbers

In Focus

Think of stories for $4 - 10 = \boxed{}$.

Let's Learn

1  's story

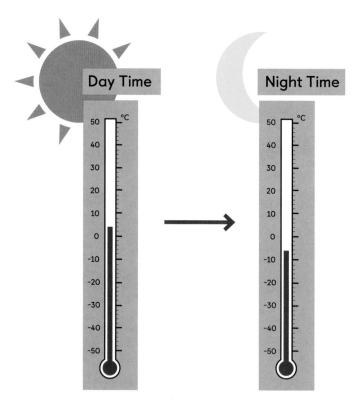

The temperature was 4 °C.
It then dropped by 10 °C.

2 's story

I took the lift from Level 4 and went 10 storeys down.

3 's story

I write £1 for each £1 I receive.

I also write £1 for each £1 I spend.

What could 's story be?

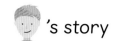

Football Results								
Team	Played	Won	Drew	Lost	Goals scored	Goals conceded	Goal difference	Result
▬	3	2	1	0	8	2	6	7
▬	3	2	0	1	7	6	1	6
▬	3	1	1	1	3	4	−1	4
▬	3	0	0	3	4	10	−6	0

Guided Practice

1 Calculate the goal difference for each team in this group.

Group A	Won	Drew	Lost	Goals scored	Goals conceded	Goal difference
▬	2	1	0	7	2	
▬	2	1	0	4	1	
▬	1	0	2	6	6	
▬	0	0	3	1	9	

Write the equation for each calculation, e.g. 7 − 2 = ☐.

Negative Numbers   Page 264

2 The water level in a well rose 3 m from −8 m.

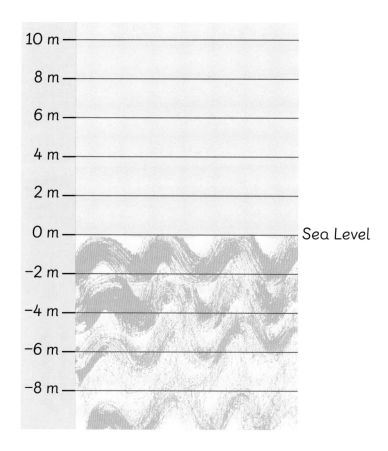

10 m
8 m
6 m
4 m
2 m
0 m — Sea Level
−2 m
−4 m
−6 m
−8 m

Is the new water level above or below sea level?

Complete Worksheet **2** – Page **183 – 184** ▶

Mind Workout ▶

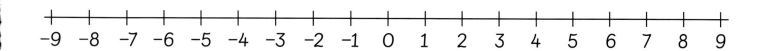

-9 -8 -7 -6 -5 -4 -3 -2 -1 0 1 2 3 4 5 6 7 8 9

Solve.

$x + 3 = 5$

$y + 3 = 3$

$z + 3 = 0$

☐ + 3 = 5

☐ + 3 = 3

Choose numbers for ☐ and ⬤ . Write a story for ☐ + ⬤ = −5

's story

Your Starter for Ten

$0 - 5 = -5$

In a quiz show, a team got the first question wrong. It got a penalty of −5 points.

If you buzz, you must answer.

I know how to...   *Self Check*

☐ add and subtract negative numbers.

☐ use negative numbers in context.

☐ solve problems involving negative numbers.